Tacita Dean: Film Works

TACITA DEAN: FILM WORKS

CHARTA

MAC@MAM

CONTENTS

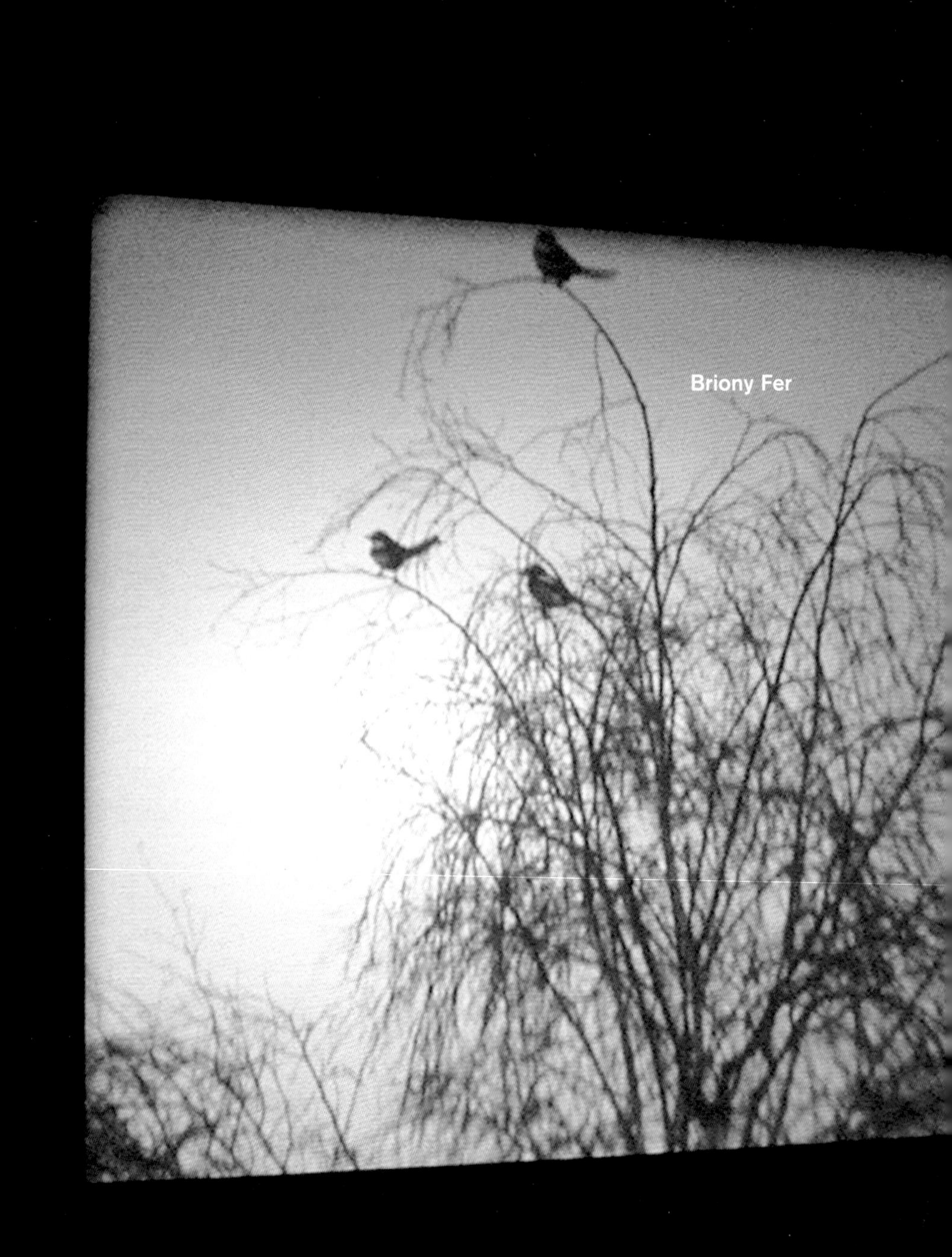

Briony Fer

A NATURAL HISTORY
OF CHANCE

"I was of three minds,
Like a tree
In which there were three blackbirds"

Wallace Stevens[1]

There seems to be very little to sustain our attention in *Pie* (2003)—just some trees, some birds, some sky. Filmed from the window of Tacita Dean's Berlin studio, the image, when rear-projected onto the wall, is not that large—about the size of a window, in fact. Nothing much happens, except, as time passes, the sun sets behind the trees. If we were waiting for something more eventful, we would be disappointed. At seven minutes, it is not a long film, but, because of the way it holds to the same view with few variations, it also requires us, as viewers, to be still—to watch, to wait, to observe. The film treads a fine line between indifference and attentiveness. On the one hand, there is the plain fact that this scene is there, to be looked at without being seen. To call it a scene, from this point of view, sounds a little too emphatic. On the other hand, as we become attuned to what we are seeing, we begin to observe what would normally fall below the threshold of our notice. A film that, at first, appears to contain very little turns out to be full of small incident: the movements of the birds in the latticework of branches, the dying light, the slow fall into semi-darkness, then into night. From seemingly not focusing on anything in particular, *Pie* comes to seem very full of the micro-movements of fluttering wings, slightly swaying branches, and birds arriving and departing.

What does it mean to think of a film like *Pie* as both empty and full at the same time? I am tempted to say that there is something contradictory about this effect, but, on reflection, I do not think "contradictory" is the right word. A better word might be "coincident," implying that emptiness and fullness co-exist with, rather than contradict, one another. *Pie* may be one of the most self-effacing of Dean's films, but it also crystallizes an effect that is characteristic of all her work. The effect derives not only from the subject, from what we observe, but from *how* we observe. It is not the absence or presence of the birds, or even the patterns of their movements, that is at stake, so much as the patterns of our viewing habits. This impinges on the larger question of narrative, but not in the narrow sense of a story depicted. On the contrary, it is as if what otherwise might quite happily travel under the name of "background," the kind of scene-setting shots used to create ambience, is prolonged and made to linger. Dean has said in relation to making this film, "I have become a birdwatcher."[2] She may not have ended up by making a nature film, but she may have created a natural history of another kind, one that is concerned with our own patterns of observation and habits of viewing. Needless to say, this is not a scientific study. Rather, it suggests that slow, patient attention to those patterns might reveal something about the nature of coincidence, not just as a trigger for recognition, but as a key structural component of cinematic experience.

Coincidence is chance's closest relative. In *Pie*, as if to make this relation concrete, there is a moment when the screen seems to undulate very slightly. It takes a while for this to register, but, when it does, it is hard to ignore. This insistent movement was a consequence of filming, but was entirely unplanned. The film was shot through an open window, and the effect was accidentally created by the heat of Dean's studio mixing with the cold air outside. Describing how she discovered the effect as the film took shape, it is clear that she relishes such chance effects. Maybe there is something seductive in the belatedness of this, the fact that it is discovered almost as an "aftereffect," but has, of course, been there from the outset, unknowingly embedded in the filmmaking process. The surface of film becomes a barely oscillating interface between inside and outside. And the materiality of film that is exposed in the just perceptibly buckling image reminds us of Dean's own intensely physical involvement with the process of making her films. She has said that she watched the magpies through her studio window as she edited on her Steenbeck inside, and it is as if both modalities of vision were imprinted on the celluloid.

By suggesting that emptiness and fullness are not necessarily incompatible, I do not mean that emptiness gives way, in the end, to a kind of plenitude. Rather there is an amplification at work that tends, if anything, to foreground the degrees of emptiness. Even the micro-incidents that fill the film and reflect back on an intense watchfulness have a certain hollowness, a refusal, at any rate, to mean something in particular. It tempts us, in thinking about Dean's work, to cut to the extraordinary web of words that envelop it. She is, herself, a very good writer, and has written a series of short, elegant texts that she has said sit alongside the work. I think we should take seriously the care with which she chooses to describe that relationship and see the value of "adjacence" as part of her work, to see the writing as coexistent, even coincident, with her films and other work, rather than as a narrative description of it.[3] Viewed in that spirit, what she writes about *Pie* is no less relevant, but differently relevant, than the film itself. What she has to say about the burden of myth and superstition that has, over centuries, attached itself to the magpie seems in an important way quite detached from the film. In order to ward off the bad luck associated with the sight of a single magpie, she puts her hand to her forehead "and mime[s] a dry spit"; others say, "Morning, Mr. Magpie, I trust your wife is well."[4] This adds another perspective, that of archaic ritual and belief. It is the unconscious fear of being seen, as if it were the birds, after all, that watch and observe *us*.

There is more than one way, then, of looking at a bird in a tree. And looking, we are never entirely immune from the anxiety of being looked back at. Everyday superstitions like this invoke ideas of the evil eye or infantile fears in general. They suggest a psychic or unconscious pattern of recognition. Irrational thoughts spill out at the sight of a magpie—or may just spill out of a film with no obvious trigger. This set of concerns form part of Dean's long-standing preoccupation with luck and chance. She has, for example, been collecting four-leafed clovers since she was a child, and she has exhibited her collection in large cases as testament to her fascination with the way the archaic survives in the smallest things, short-circuiting the instrumental logic of cause and effect. Yet the magpies in *Pie* are not symbols or harbingers of doom, at least not in the conventional sense. *Pie* does not operate as iconography, each object a symbol for something else. If chance is at work, it is as strategy, rather than simply as subject. The more explicit references to luck or superstition merely stress the pivotal role she has given to less nameable chance effects and encounters between things.

Coincidences happen in the absence of a causal explanation. They occur where two or more "events" co-exist, without reason, in the same pocket of time or space. It is only their concurrence that connects them. Mere coincidence is the flip-side of destiny or fate. The sheer risk of chance is that there is no predestined narrative already in place on which to rely. Although it may seem to contradict the meticulous care with which Dean makes her films, a receptiveness to chance events has become an important part of her working method. To marshal such coincidences is, of course, deliberately to make something out of them. Much of Dean's own account of her films makes use of this literary trope. When she went to the Cayman Islands to make *Teignmouth Electron* (1999), a film based on Donald Crowhurst's trimaran, she found the "bubble house," which became the subject of another work. When she went to Madagascar in order to see a total eclipse of the sun, she was also "lured there by a fleeting remark on an eclipse-watcher's website saying that those of us who made it as far as Morombe might also stand a chance of seeing the green ray."[5] Equally coincidentally, she found out the evening before she left that Eric Rohmer had faked the light effect in his 1986 film *Le Rayon Vert.* And the list goes on. The chain of events is potentially infinite. It is not a dream narrative, although it has a certain oneiric quality. To me, it feels like thinking, where thought is almost tangible in its materiality. This is thought at the border of the daydream, where it may swerve off course at any moment, triggering further thoughts. This process connects powerfully to the fractured narratives of W.G. Sebald, a writer Dean greatly admires.[6] Rather than compare them, I think it is more accurate to see their work as "coincident" in the way I have been trying to describe. These points of connection, where disparate thoughts touch, and then trail off, are also points of *dis*connection. These frictions also fill the gaps between Dean's writing and her films, and they animate, too, the intervals and spaces *between* the films. This is another reason why, for all the lingering shots she uses in her work, her films are very far from still or contemplative.

This is a way of thinking in which links and disconnections do not rule each other out, but feed off each other. There is nothing more resonant of this than the name of Donald Crowhurst's boat. *Teignmouth Electron* brings together a rather quaint, old-fashioned, seaside resort on the south coast of England and the science-fiction future that could once be encapsulated in the term "electron," which now seems more resonant of a school physics lesson. Crowhurst was a Sunday sailor who entered the 1968 'round-the-world yacht race. Even when English men did go to sea in sports jackets and ties like Crowhurst, Teignmouth was an unlikely place to set out on a circumnavigation of the globe. Crowhurst's is a true story of epic failure. His trimaran, designed to up-to-the-minute specifications, failed even to keep the water out of its hatches across the English Channel, let alone the great seas of the Southern Ocean. In a tragic personal journey, Crowhurst fast realized that he was not going to make it, so, rather than withdraw from the race and risk humiliation and ruin, he fabricated a second, fictitious log in addition to the one that actually recorded his position and pottered around in the South Atlantic, hoping to join the race again on its final leg. The made-up log grew increasingly incoherent, ending up quite dazzlingly so, and Crowhurst jumped overboard. His body was never found.

Strikingly, the film *Teignmouth Electron* is *not* the story of Donald Crowhurst. For all the seductiveness of his story, narrated by Dean in a parallel text, in which she stresses his fall into what is known, she says, as "time-madness amongst sailors,"[7] the film centers on the ruined hull of Crowhurst's trimaran lying stranded on a beach in the Caymans, as if entranced by it to the exclusion of everything else. There is a striking simplicity to the anti-narrative of the scene of a boat rotting on a beach. It gives the impression of having been washed up, even though its current owner actually put it there. Dean deliberately absents the "story," or narrative of events leading up to the boat simply being there, from the film. Or, perhaps more accurately, fragments of the story get remaindered there. When, after some delay the camera lingers over the name *Teignmouth Electron* painted on the hull, the full pathos (or is it absurd self-aggrandizement?) of the endeavor is inserted into the film's structure, as if its memory has only belatedly surfaced. There is something very matter-of-fact about the presence of the trimaran, touched by the events that brought it there, but absolutely not "about" the man to whom those events happened. And, although the whole story of Crowhurst's fictitious log prompts us to question the blurring of fact and fiction in Dean's films, it is precisely the plotting of her own journey, rather than Crowhurst's, that we follow. When the small plane surges upwards at the end, the camera still filming, the reverberations are even further removed, not least, as various commentators have noted, because the movement echoes the vertiginous ascent of Robert Smithson's helicopter spiraling noisily above his *Spiral Jetty* in the Utah salt lake. If the trimaran stands as a monument to anything, I would say it is to the missing narratives that touch upon, but are ultimately severed from, the film that we see. The "thingness" of the trimaran, the awkward shape of its three peeling hulls—with holes through which water now drips—is very far from the streamlining we might associate with a boat built for racing. It looks more like the outer shell of a giant crustacean, beached and decaying. The shell-like structure of the trimaran (or, for that matter, the bubble house) seems to reflect back on the way narrative functions in Dean's work. Narrative content is not to be found inside the films, but always in some tangential relation to them, as if film itself becomes some kind of empty shell or leaking vessel.

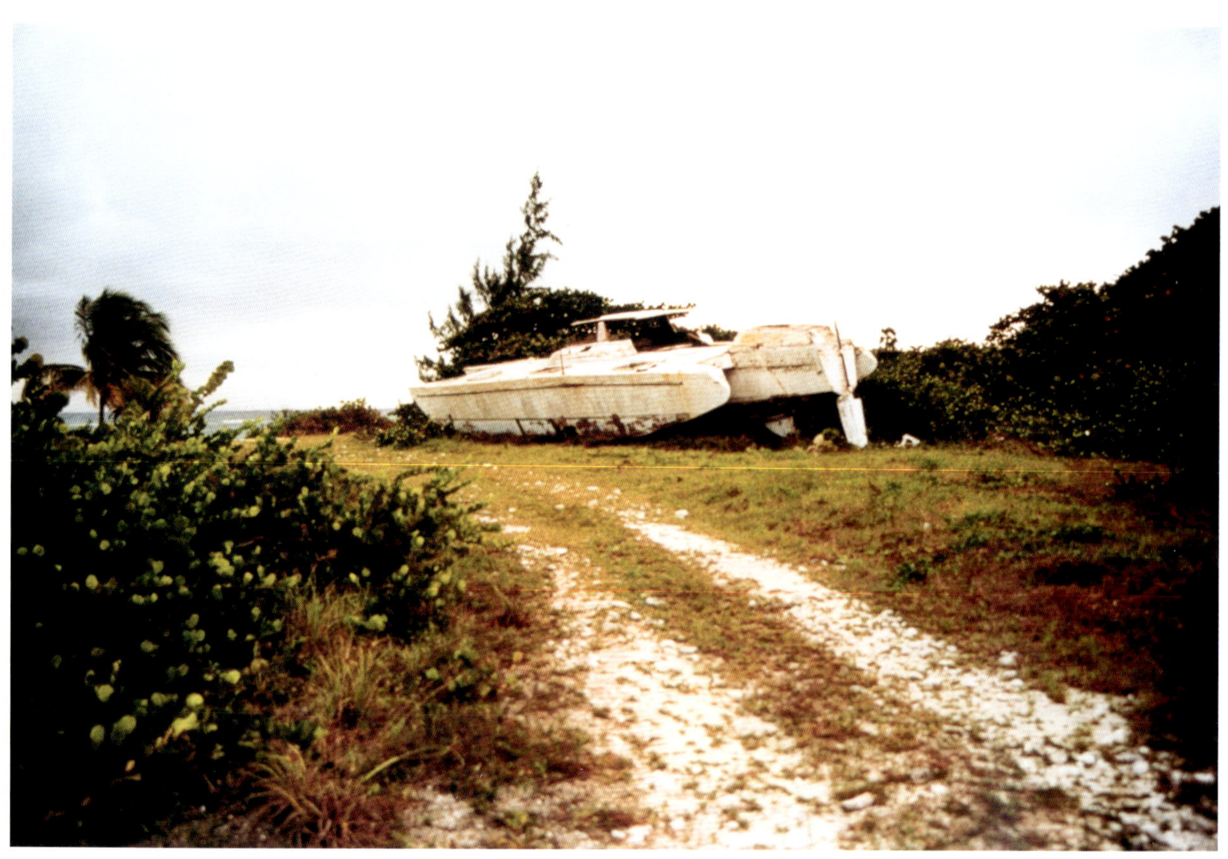

Teignmouth Electron, Cayman Brac, C-prints, 27 1/8 x 35 inches

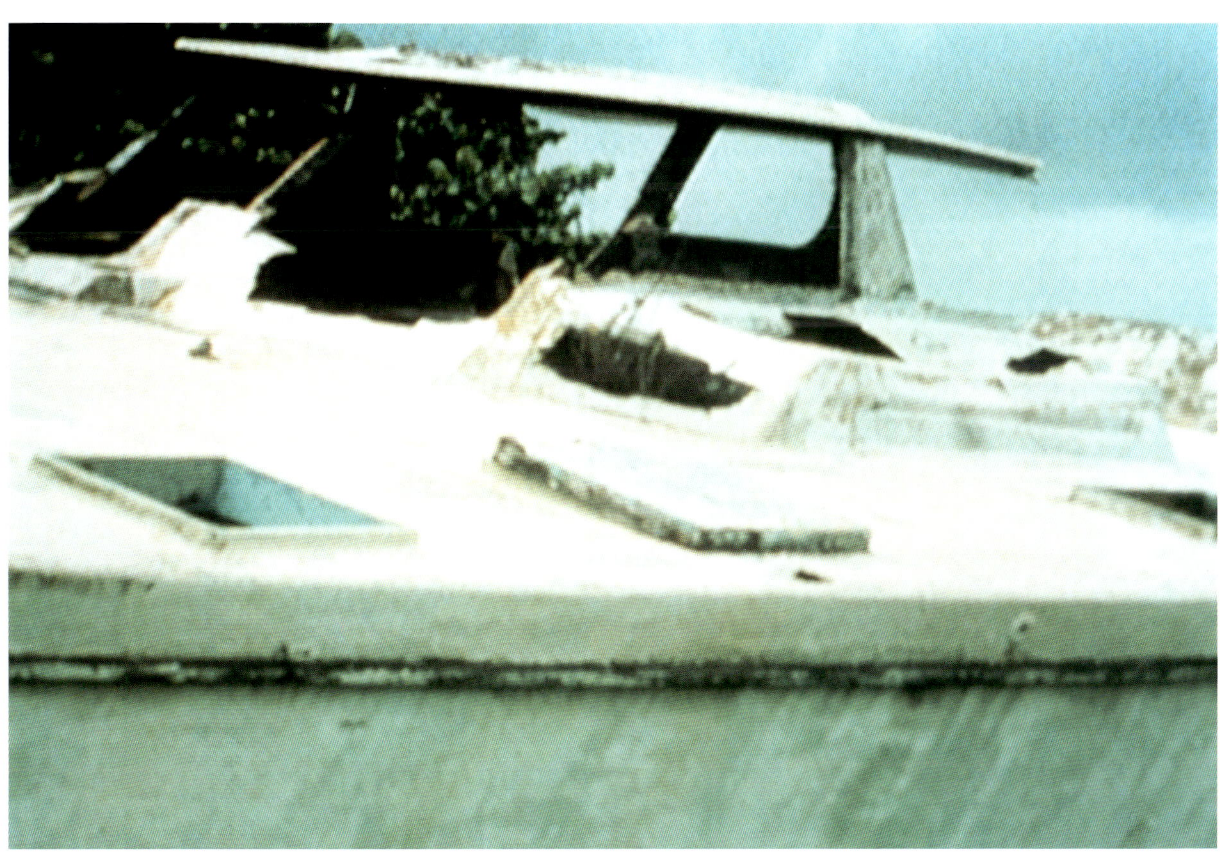

One of Roland Barthes's brilliantly concise essays in *Mythologies*, published in the early 1950s, called "The *Nautilus* and the Drunken Boat," compares Jules Verne's travel imagination, which Barthes saw as an "exploration of closure," and Arthur Rimbaud's extraordinary poem "Le Bateau ivre," in which the boat "becomes a travelling eye" and which represents a "genuine poetics of exploration."[8] Verne, says Barthes, "had an obsession for plenitude: he never stopped putting a last touch to the world and furnishing it, making it full with an egg-like fullness."[9] The difference is starkly drawn between the fantasy of a ship, which, like a moving house, is all about enclosedness (all the more so because of its long journey around the entire globe), and the radical dissolution of language in Rimbaud's poem (notwithstanding the fact that Rimbaud had never seen the sea when he wrote it and relied on writers such as Verne for his image of it). But more than the image of the boat itself, the "ecstatic flotsam" of the language marks the vessel's disintegration and, for Barthes, the difference between an open system and a closed one. That is to say, the gaping holes in a porous narrative structure do not only describe an event that is external to us, but describe something about ourselves as subjects. Despite the fact that some of Dean's chalkboard drawings of ships so strongly suggest the original illustrations of Verne's novels, I think the disjunctions in her work powerfully refuse the kind of narrative plenitude that Barthes criticized in Verne. The kind of fullness I have been describing in her work is more likely to seep out than to be sealed in.

Nowhere is this more apparent than in her use of sound. There is a moment in the mid-1990s when Dean gives up using her own voice, as she had done as voice-over in films such as *A Bag of Air* (1995).[10] Far from marking an abandonment of sound, this decisive moment marks the beginning of a far more radical exploration of its possibilities. She became interested in the kind of sound that sound engineers usually edit out, what might be called background noise. Interestingly, although much has been made, rightly, of her attachment to 16mm film and her rejection of the digital image-world, she uses digital sound. Whatever else this says, it shows a pragmatic stand, as if the best and most effective way to deliver the crude, archaic quality of everyday sound is only by using digital, post-production means. In *Pie*, for example, the soundtrack consists of traffic noise mixed with birdsong. This is the kind of soundtrack with which we live all the time, the normal interference of everyday life. The scene may be of "nature," but the experience is insistently urban (and magpies have colonized urban habitats in recent years). In *Palast* (2004), the sounds of barely heard conversations mingle with the sound of traffic. The sun may be setting in gorgeous, golden tones reflected on the façade of a building, but this is what a city sounds like. Writing in a house in London, this is the ambient noise that I do not notice I am hearing—the sound of birds, an airplane overhead, the kind of noise that means it is never silent.

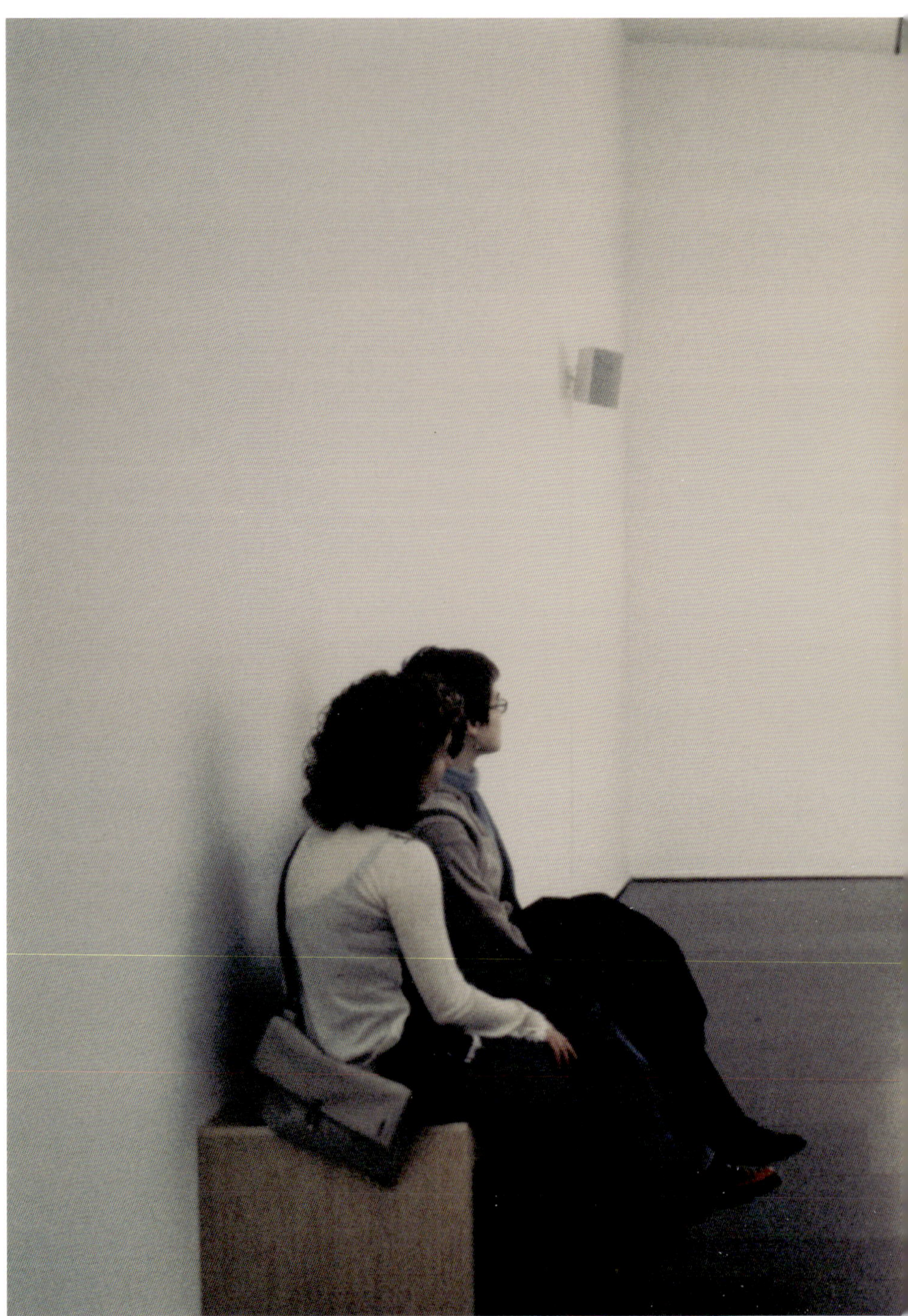

A Bag of Air (Installation at Museu d'Art Contemporani de Barcelona)

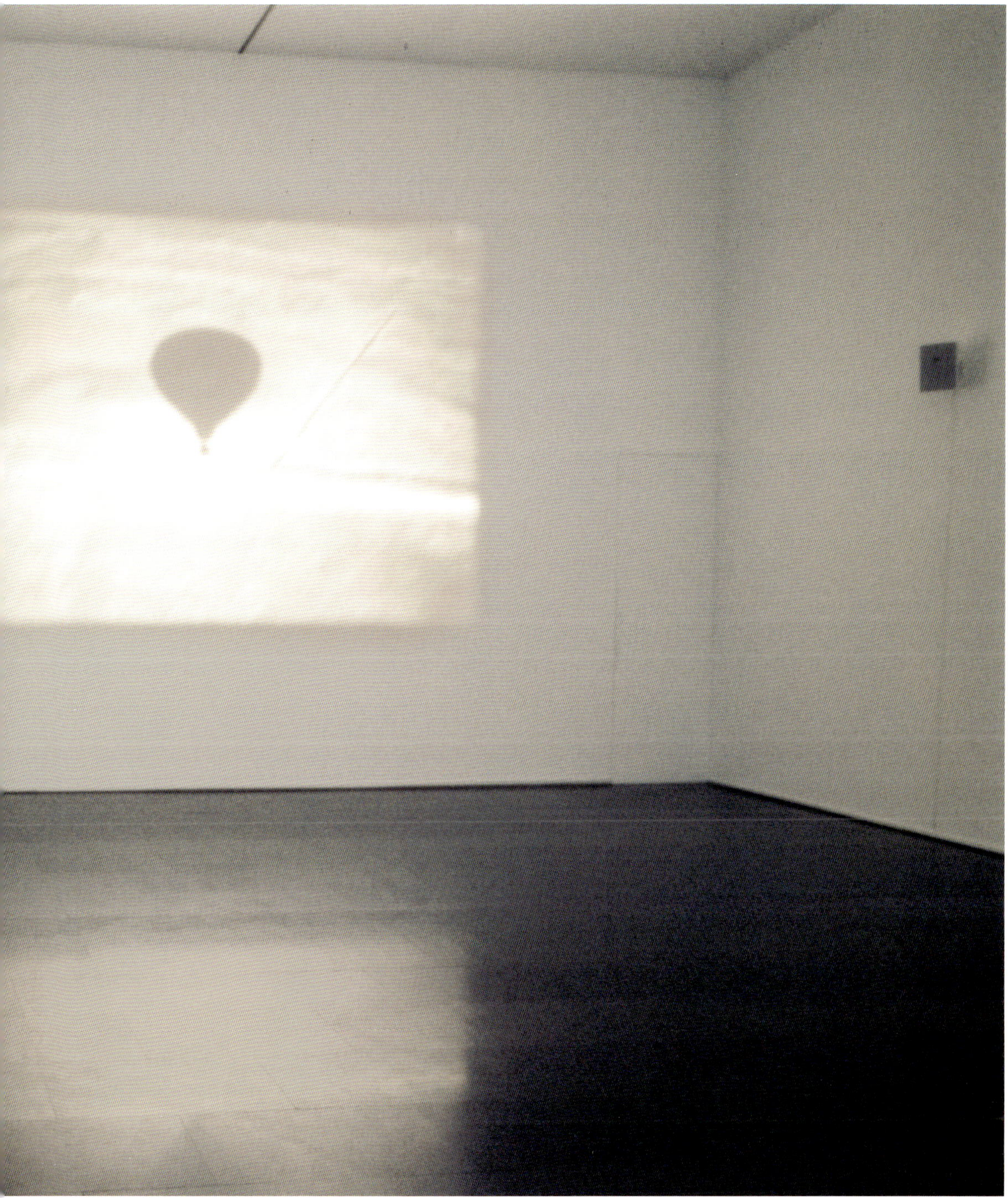

If the film of *Teignmouth Electron* could itself be regarded as a leaking vessel, emptied of narrative, then *Sound Mirrors* (1999) "leaks" sound. The giant concrete structures were built after the First World War as the first line of England's defenses, designed to pick up the sound of enemy aircraft before they were visible to sight. Dean has called them "giant ears."[11] They represent the prehistory of radar, although they never worked and have long been left abandoned on the now flooded shingle strand at Denge, next to Dungeness in Kent, on the south coast of England. This is the largest shingle habitat for wildlife in Europe and, whilst not actually that isolated, feels remote in time. The structures possess a brooding stillness, but one far from silent. Though muted, the film is full of fractured, intermittent sounds, which include not only birdsong (the place is now a nature reserve), but the sound of small aircraft taking off and landing at the small airstrip that lies alongside the site. Lydd airport once transported rich English vacationers with their cars to Le Touquet in France, but it is now well past its heyday and mainly used by amateur pilots in small private planes (although there are plans afoot to turn it into a new international airport). Dean once said that Chris Marker's 1962 film *La Jetée* made her think of Lydd airport. She has also talked of Marker's soundtrack of muffled whisperings.[12] The idea of a collage of sounds, where sounds are as material as any image, is clearly important in all Dean's work, as if the low-level noise of everyday life were literally collected from the world. This is reminiscent of a short story by J.G. Ballard called "The Sound-Sweep," which looks to a time when so-called ultra-sonic music has rendered the human voice redundant and when sound-sweeps are employed to "hoover up" the debris of leftover sounds, the remains of human voices and conversations. Dean's hybrid soundtracks, which often import noises from "elsewhere," that is to say, from outside the field pictured in the projected image, also powerfully undermine the idea of plenitude in favor of a much more frenetic, if low-key, sense of what Ballard called "psychosemantics."[13]

Much has been made of Dean's interest in the work of Robert Smithson. Dungeness—as a kind of desert-on-sea—could be seen as England's answer to the sites of Smithson's dystopian vision. *Sound Mirrors*, I suppose, could even be seen as an aural equivalent to his *Yucatan Mirror Displacements*, mirrors placed in the landscape at oblique angles, in which "scraps of sight accumulated until the eyes were engulfed by scrambled reflections."[14] Certainly Smithson represents the model of an artist who did not just write about his work, but made writing an essential part of his work, and, as such, is of huge importance for Dean and for many other artists. But, in a sense, while clearly true, the comparisons with Smithson also miss the point. It is not only Dean's move away from voice-over narration that differentiates her use of sound. And while echoes of Smithson, like the helicopter that I have already mentioned, exist in her work, I think Dean's approach is far closer to Ballard's idea of "sound debris." The low burr of small planes accelerating or fading out in *Sound Mirrors* provides a sound envelope that we, as viewers, occupy. The interwoven sounds generate another kind of rhythm, one that seems to coincide more closely with the way thoughts often trail off or veer away. Perhaps the most significant element within that sound-envelope is the noise of the whirring projector in the gallery, with which the soundtrack both competes and mingles. The presence of the sound-envelope that Dean constructs means that it is not only the concrete structures themselves, but the whole artwork, that becomes a kind of expanded, reverberating "sound mirror."

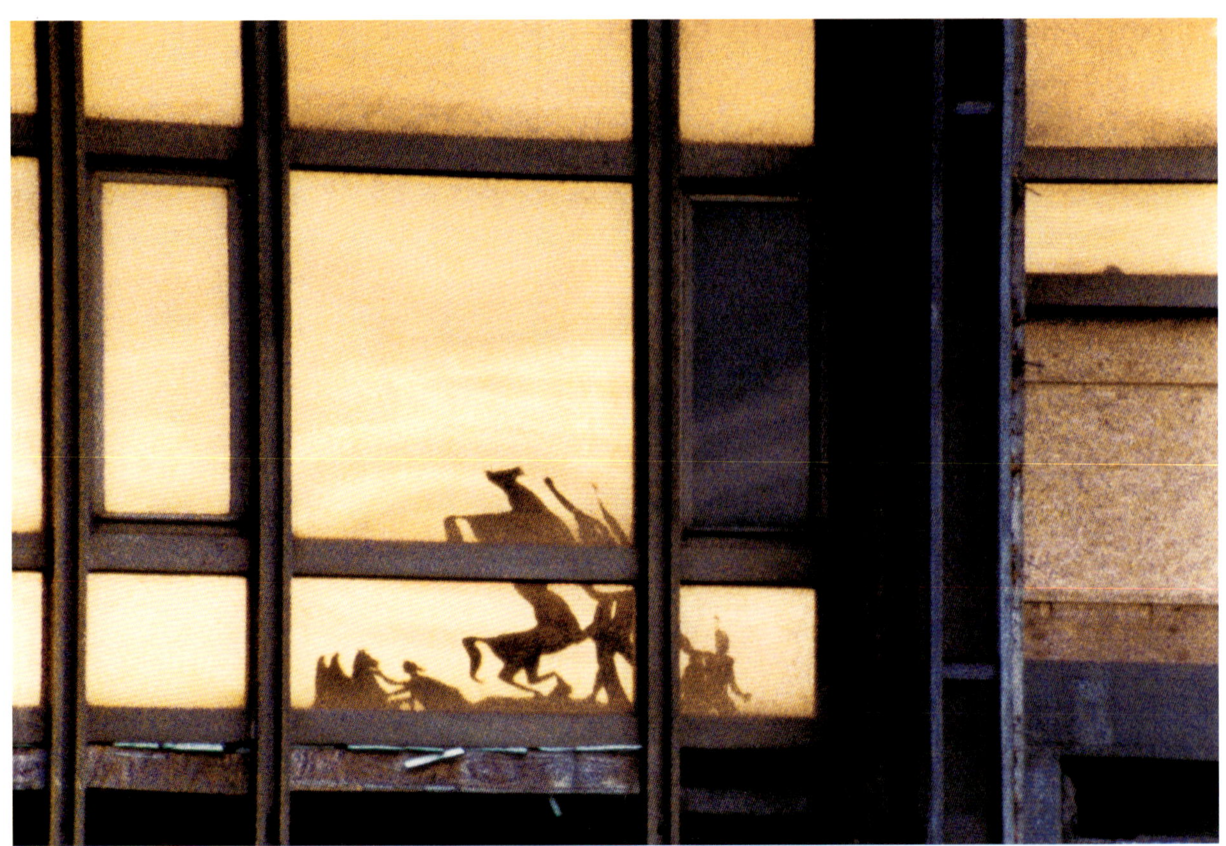

Palast

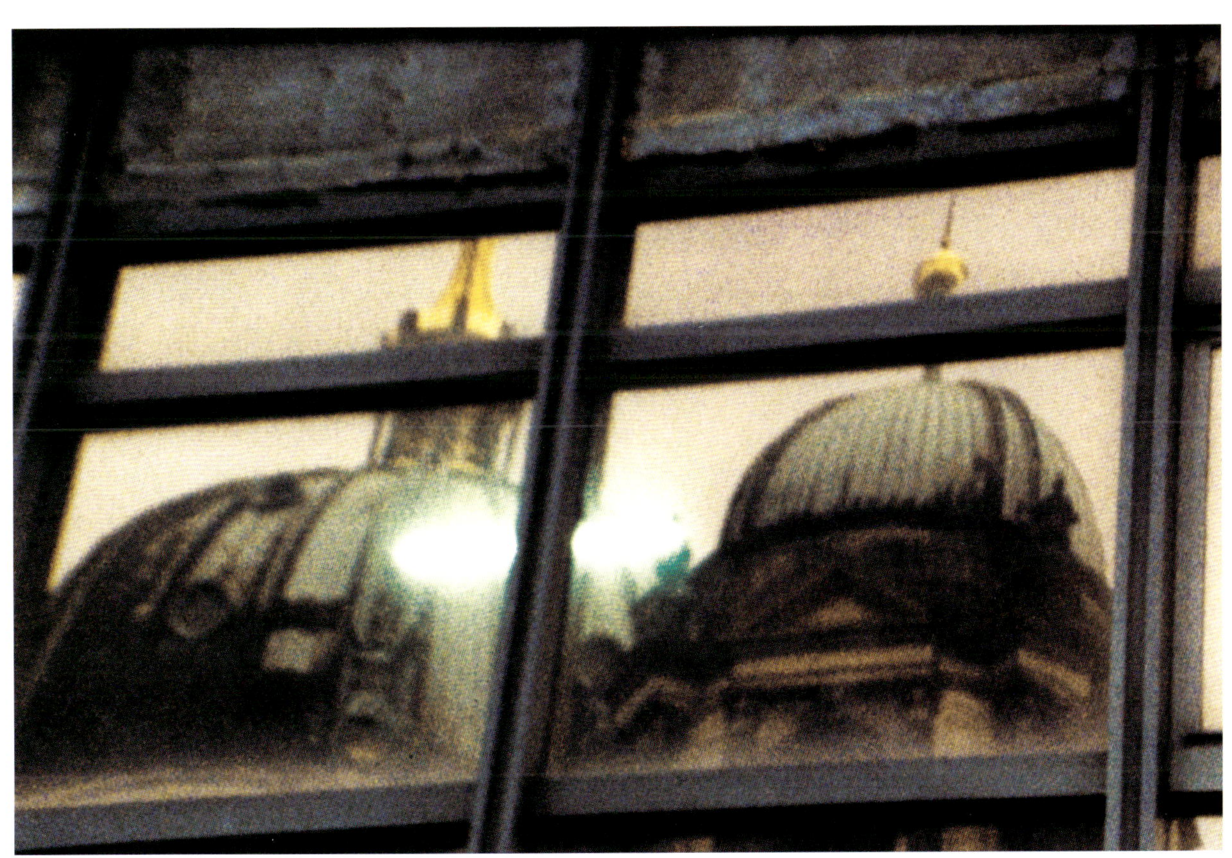

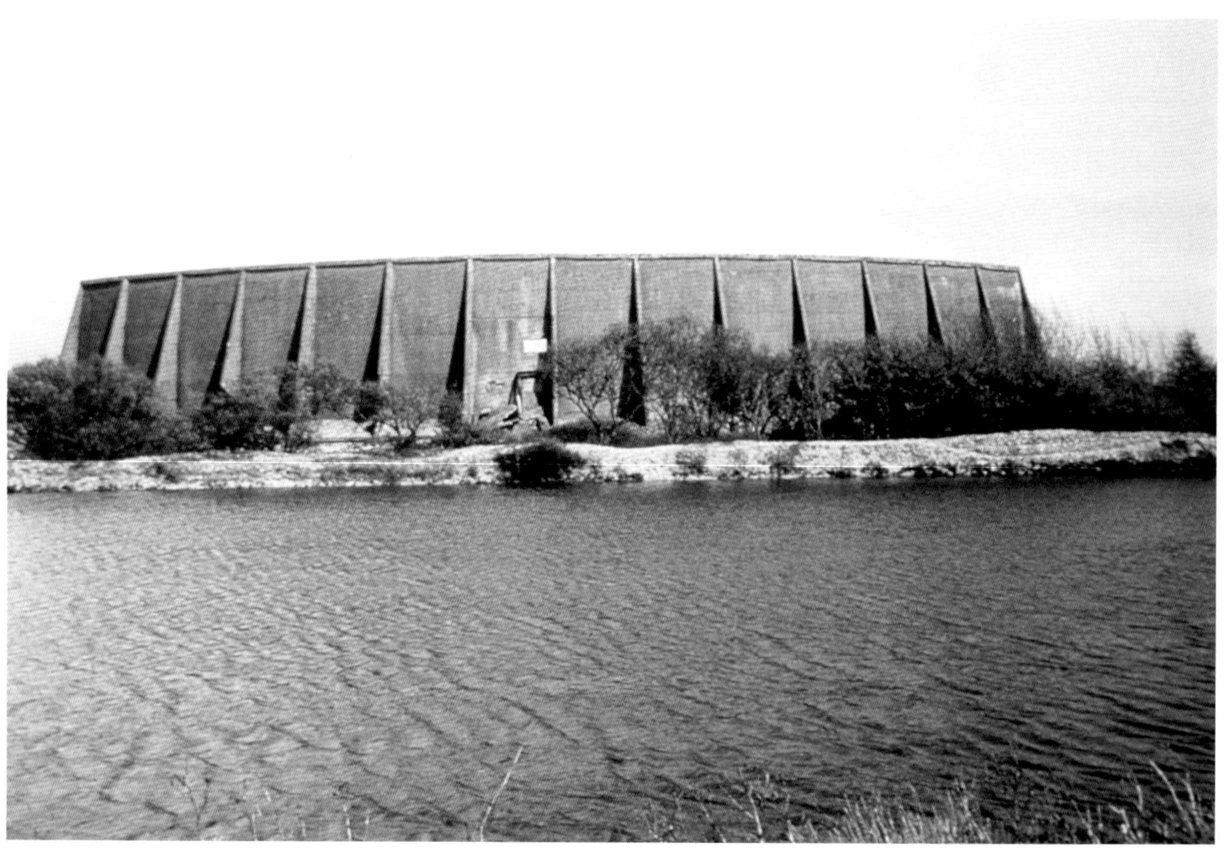

Sound Mirrors

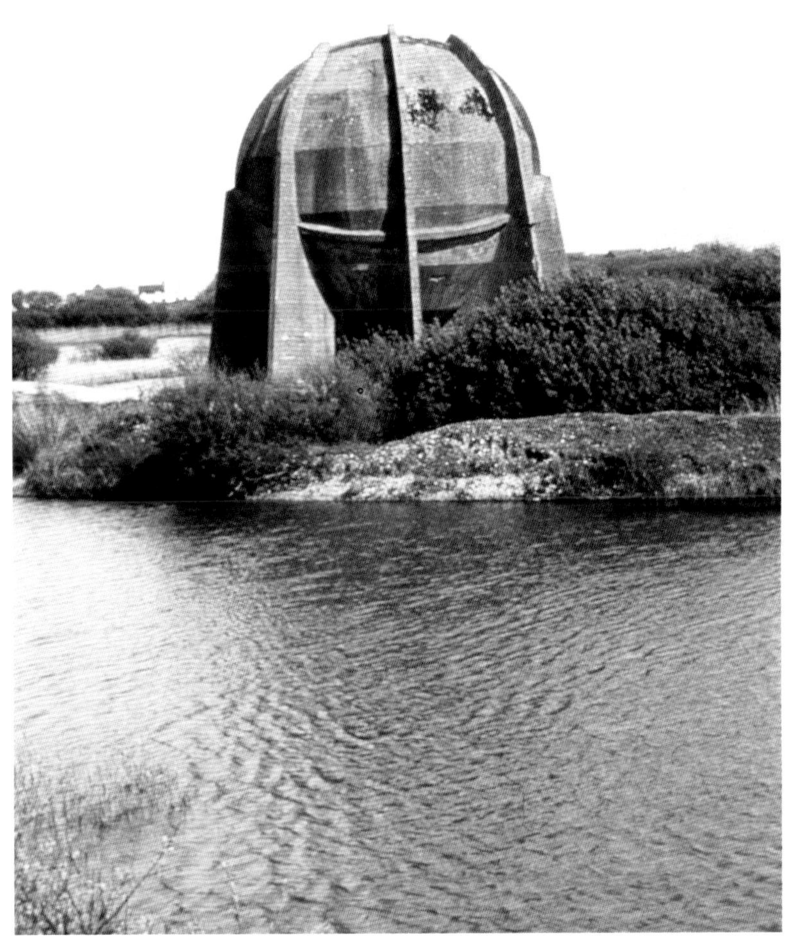

We can see this kind of self-reflexivity as part of Dean's long preoccupation with the structure of film, but also with the phenomenological aspect of the cinematic experience and the sheer corporeality of the world of celluloid. Watching her films, the space between the screen and the projector becomes a frenetic and charged place. The long static shots are counteracted by the speed of the film, visible in the occasional striations and marks on the celluloid as it passes noisily through the projector. Celluloid has an intensely sensual quality, especially its slight imperfections, its flickering surface an antidote to the bleakness of any subject. *Sound Mirrors* may be in black-and-white, but, as night falls, it becomes more luminescent, rather than less. In Dean's color films, often as the light dies the most ravishing light effects are revealed. In *Palast*, the sound of traffic noise mixes with the muffled, incomprehensible sound of human voices, and the setting sun is caught in the copper-clad façade of the former People's Palace in Berlin. The film acts as a kind of receptacle in which the screen is filled with the grid of the building's structure but also with the remarkable light of the sun. Dean has talked about the building as a kind of "light-trap," a glinting, reflective surface amidst the gray of Berlin.[15] This could equally describe the film itself, as the golden light filling the screen is made even more jewel-like by the small size of the work. The film becomes its own "light-trap" for us as viewers.

The People's Palace, a leftover from the Communist era, is now being demolished. Dean is clearly fascinated with what is about to become, or which has already become, obsolete; the medium of 16mm film, of course, has been seen as the about-to-be-lost object par excellence.[16] A melancholic impulse, an undertow of yearning, seems to pervade all her work. But there is also a counter-movement, and it is this that I want to stress. Drawing on Julia Kristeva's vocabulary, we could think of it in terms of art's capacity to act as a "counter-depressant."[17] At the very least, I think, Dean's work is *alive* to loss. One of the films that most clearly shows this is *Gellért* (1998). Filmed in a spa in Budapest, old women taking the waters seem to occupy a space of limbo between life and death. There is something haunting in their pale white bodies, partly shrouded in white aprons, moving through the faded grandeur of the spa interior. They could almost be shades as they move between the pools, at times rising from, at times descending into, the waters. But, at the same time there is a very strong sense of the physicality of these fleshy, lived-in, ordinary bodies. The architectural space they occupy echoes the double-action. On the one hand, it seems almost subterranean, encasing these bodies and entombing them. But then, in the next moment, there seems something remarkably light in their movements, as if the pungent blue-green depths of the whole space, and not just the pools in which they wallow, could be underwater. What does it feel like to live in a body? Not unlike this I would say. Against the deathly torpor of *Gellért*, there exists an exhilaration in the communality of these women, who sit about and chat or move about in groups.[18] And there is nothing melancholic about the way in which this watery, weightless place seems to open the body to the possibility of freedom. It may only be temporary, but should not be underestimated.

Having begun with *Pie*, perhaps the simplest of Dean's films, I shall end with one of her most sensual and complex films to date. *Kodak* (2006) brings together many of the ideas about which I have been talking, but also makes us think again about the earlier films. In an accompanying text, Dean recounts how, in an age of digital photography, analogue film has become out-of-date and already almost forgotten. The Kodak factory at Chalon-sur-Saône in France, where it was filmed, has ceased production of analogue film altogether now and the only film still being produced there is X-ray film. As she describes it, there is something revelatory in that moment of disappearance: "From a viscous blue solid to an evanescent transparency, the manufacture of film is a journey of sublime beauty, and one I would never have known were it not for its incipient obsolescence."[19] This is a powerful narrative, and it dramatizes the passionate attachment to celluloid that has increasingly come to animate all her work. She has cast other films she has made in similar terms. Most vividly, for example, she described how, in one of her shortest films, *The Green Ray* (at two and a half minutes, the length of a single reel), the processing revealed "in a single frame of celluloid" a green ray that had "proved itself too elusive for the pixellation of the digital world."[20] At that moment, she was not exactly sure whether or not she saw the mythic green ray, the very last ray of the setting sun as it falls below the horizon line, of which she had gone in search on her Madagascan journey. Where others had failed to record it using video, the magic of celluloid was to capture and materialize (belatedly) that infinitesimal moment.

Kodak begins in black-and-white with a series of deadpan shots of the factory interior. Incorporating sequences of black-and-white and color, it follows the process of making film through the factory (its "journey," as Dean puts it, linking it to all the other journeys she has filmed). It shows, in a matter-of-fact way, the material transformation of film as it moves through the production process. It documents the different stages of manufacture: rolling over casters, being swathed in polyethylene, pressed into sheets. If film had always been the medium of choice for reflecting early twentieth-century dreams of a technological future, now analogue film marks its own swan song. *Kodak* recalls the materialist visions of the historical avant-garde, in which artists such as Aleksandr Rodchenko, in photography, and Dziga Vertov, in film, would take their cameras to the factory to film the material facts, as they saw it, of production, which meant filming not individual workers but the things themselves, in close-up and from unusual angles. With the human protagonists cut out, the objects and machinery formed part of a heroic new vision of modernity. Dean reveals the production process as the undoing of that utopian vision. Then, the "camera-eye" marked out the future; now, in a reverse movement, it marks its own death. The Kodak factory, which was once on the edge of technological advance, is now itself a kind of relic from the past. In this sense, like the architectural relic featured in *Bubble House* (1999), it recalls a future that was—the kind of future that was imaginable and that looked like this in the 1960s, but does not look like it any longer. The factory interior, with its panels of controls and white-overalled technicians, recalls a spaceship, just as the bubble house does, but it is unclear whether it has landed or is stranded there in bleak isolation. *Kodak*'s hermetically sealed environment, forming a network of internal spaces and corridors, recalls the complex inner worlds of movies like Andrei Tarkovsky's *Solaris* and Stanley Kubrick's *2001: A Space Odyssey*.

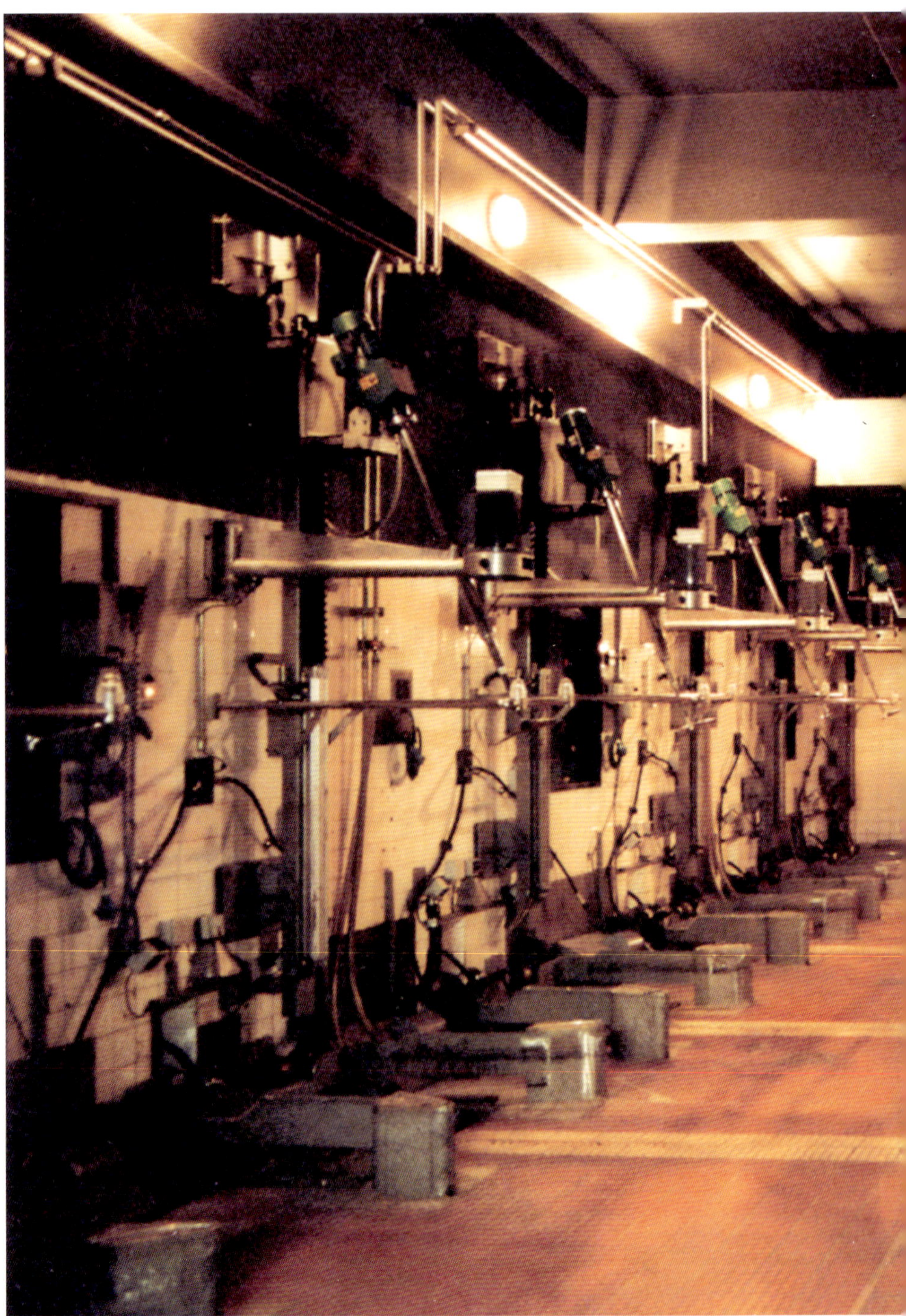

Kodak

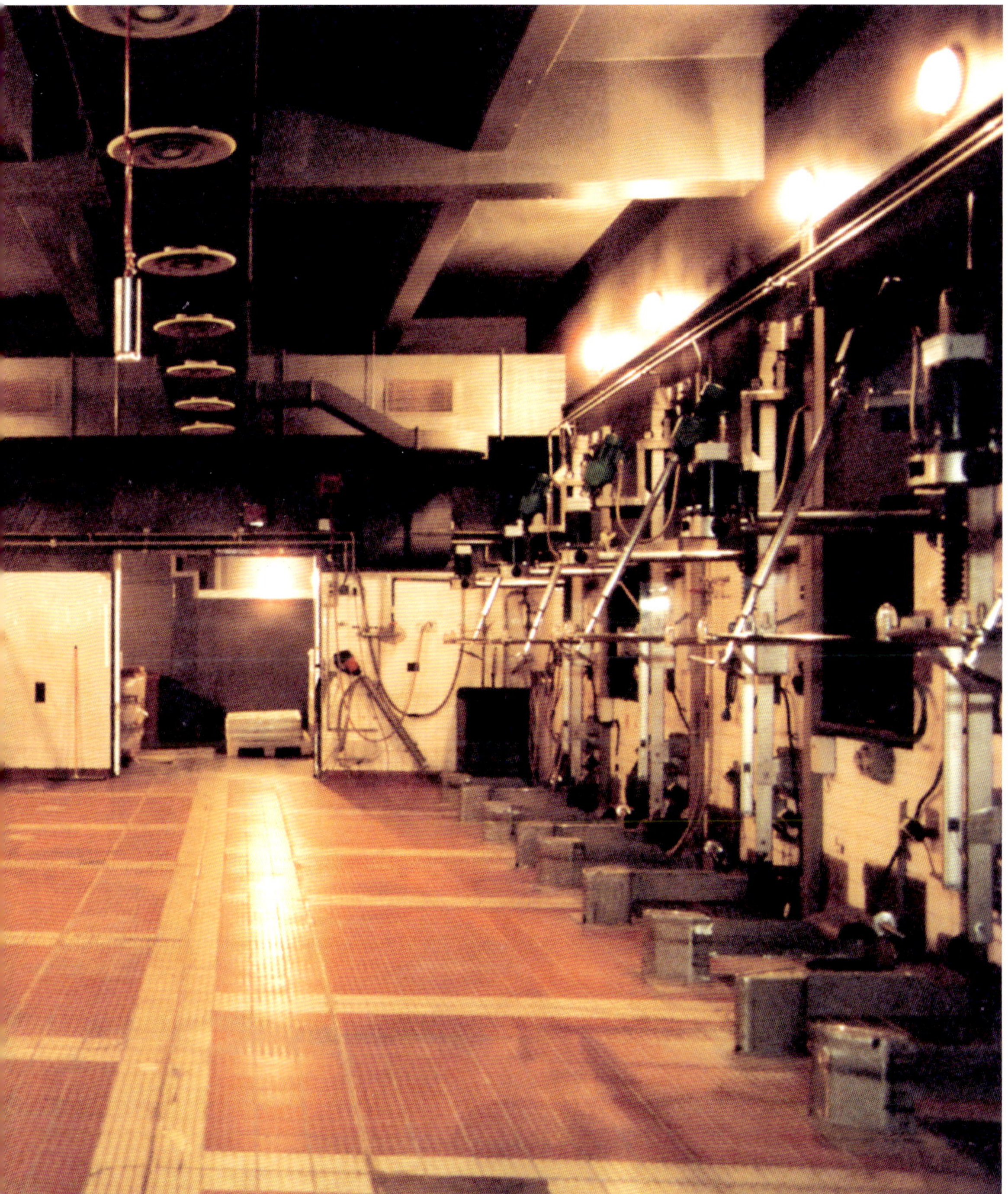

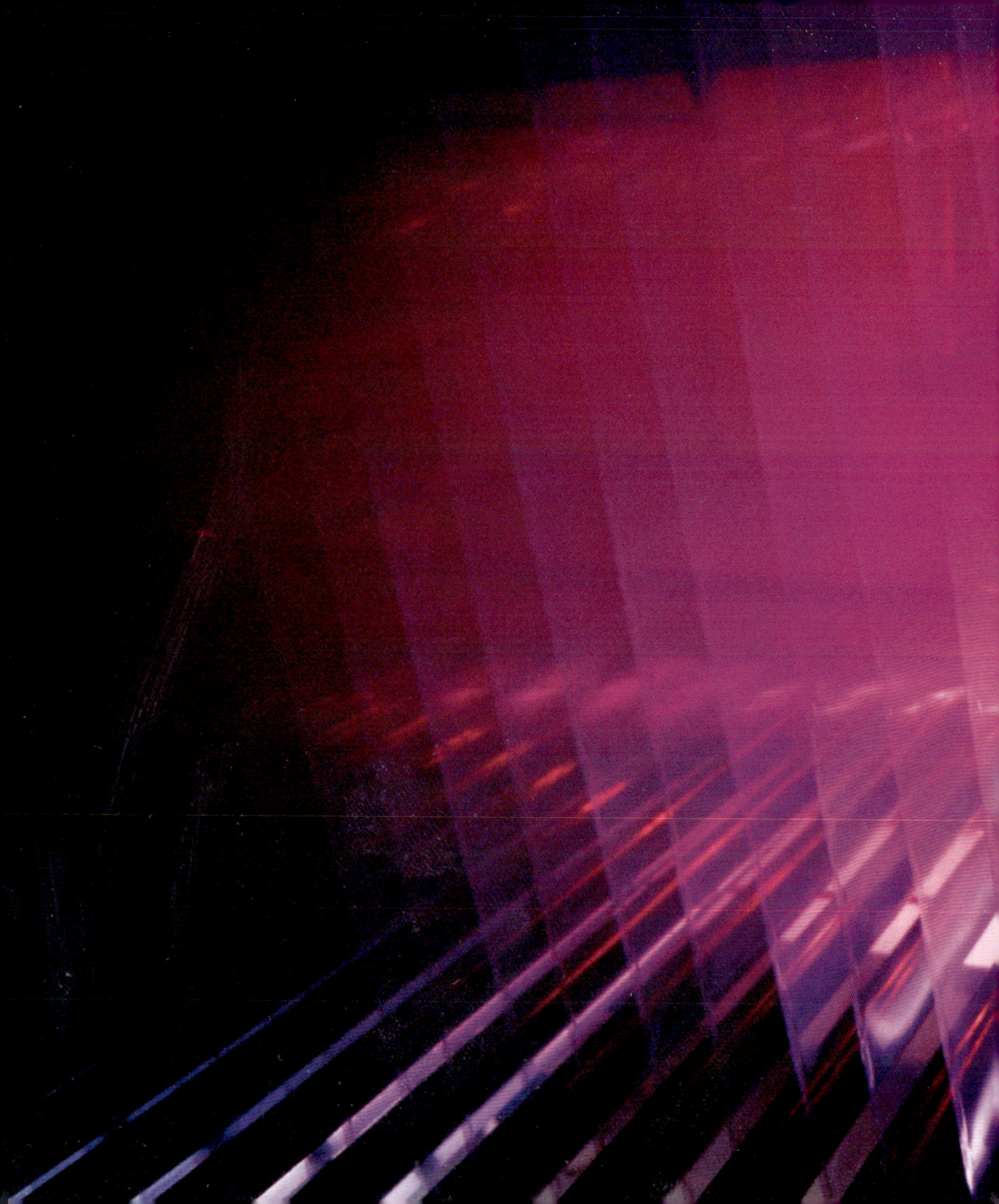

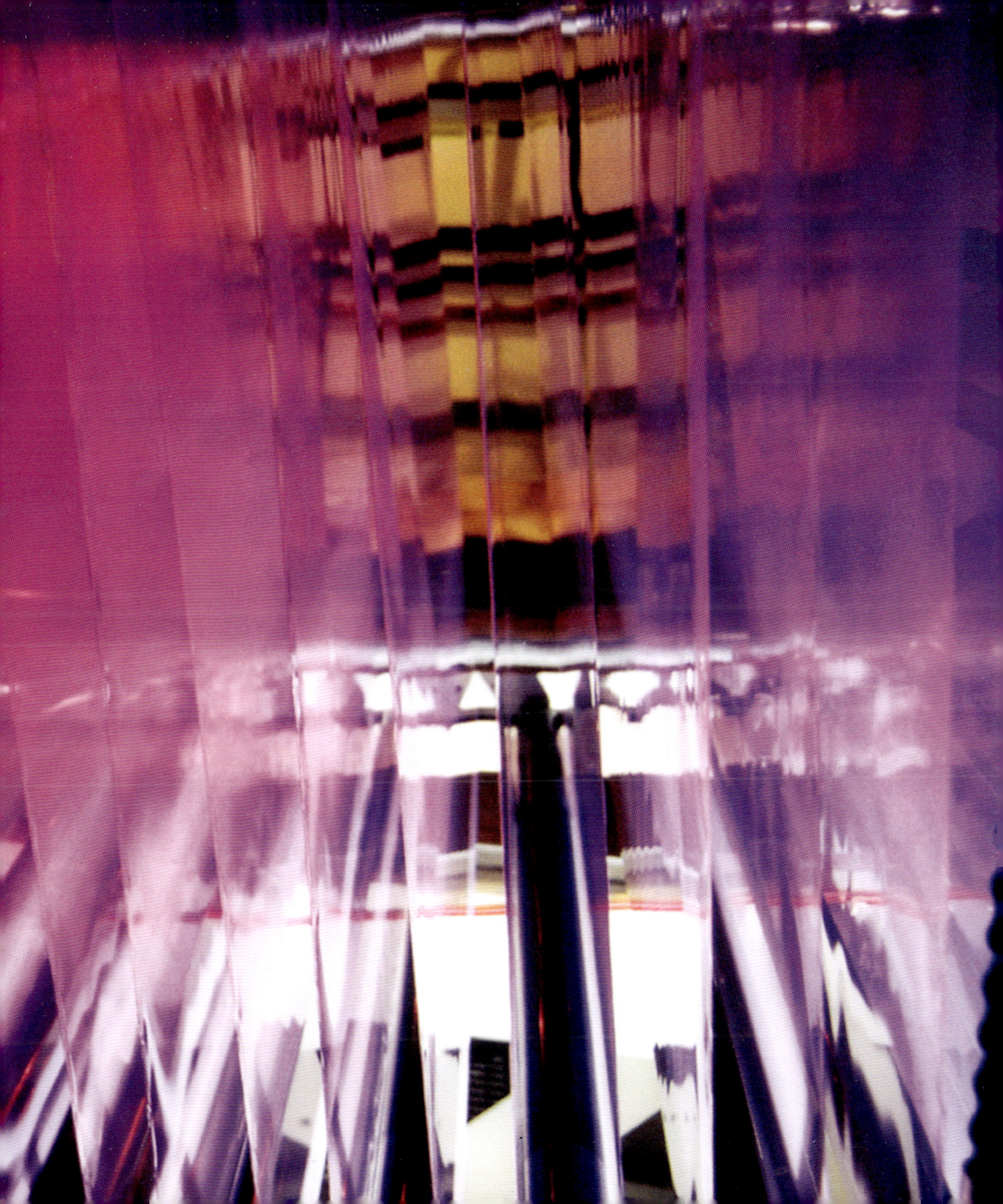

When, early in *Kodak*, the transition to color comes, it is not overly dramatic; a spool of film turns to color, almost imperceptibly. The shift between color and black-and-white films looks back to Tarkovsky, who famously interspersed them. But it is the way Dean works with color that is so striking here. Out of the somber and clinical factory environment, color erupts in ways that seem quite unanticipated by her earlier films. These sequences feature extraordinary chromatic effects. Suddenly the film is blue, shot through with light, then blue coalesces with green. Later, a shimmering pink of the celluloid sheets more or less fills the entire screen, making it hard to keep track of the logic of the production process. These interludes seem far more abstract than anything Dean had done previously. Whether or not she had in mind the abstract color tableaux that appear at intervals in Kubrick's film, the way color figures in *Kodak* absolutely does not fix a formal structure or pattern in place. Kubrick is more like Jules Verne, whereas Dean's color is more like Rimbaud's delirious excess, dissolving the image rather than keeping it in place.

In these moments, it may seem as if *Kodak* makes a dazzling spectacle out of the production of film in the modern factory. But just as this "journey of sublime beauty" is documented, the effects of color—its porosity—undo the very logic of the image that underpins that spectacle of production. That is to say, the social efficacy of the ideal factory—like the seaworthiness of the ideal boat in Rimbaud's poem—is hardly the point. Color becomes a kind of resistant material that at various points fails to keep the surface of the screen intact. Dean's sense of color is complex. Near the end of the film, she reverts to black-and-white to film the abandoned part of the factory where the debris of tangled strips of film is strewn across the floor, but still the film cuts back and forth, and the final shot is in color. It is not as if black-and-white film is the only vehicle or language of loss. On the contrary, color, in what I see as the most radical innovation, becomes the means of the film's own ruination. I am reminded here of Derek Jarman's book *Chroma*, which the film director and artist wrote on color when he was dying of AIDS in his beloved Dungeness. There are all sorts of ways that Jarman represents an important figure for Dean. It was he, she has written, who persuaded her that it was possible to make work out of the Kent marshlands, the landscape of her childhood.[21] In *Chroma*, as blindness engulfs him, Jarman writes of the "shaky shimmer of petrol patterns on a puddle" and "the iridescence [which] brings back childhood."[22] Jarman's color-scapes succinctly sum up what it might mean to be alive to loss, in the sense that I have suggested marks the generative impulse in Dean's work.

Kodak is a sustained reflection on color. And, as such, it forces us to think again about the significance of Dean's approach to color in her other films, in particular her fascination with setting suns. Sunsets, of course, are among the most spectacular disappearing acts provided by nature. They mark time through the gradations of fading light. These endings will be endlessly repeated. But they are also about color as a means of film's dissolution. As early as *Disappearance at Sea* (1996), color works as a kind of "ecstatic flotsam." In *Palast*, the colored light of the sunset, caught in the reflective surface of the building's façade—a geometric grid that fills the screen—seems equally "ecstatic." The editing does not create the illusion of a seamless fall into night, but instead appears fractured, as if watching time pass were necessarily discontinuous. (In this respect, it is unlike the way darkness falls relentlessly and barely noticeably over the Empire State Building in Andy Warhol's famous eight-hour epic *Empire* [1964].) And, whereas the ravishing effects of color had previously tended to be concentrated outside, like the view through the windows of the revolving tower in *Fernsehturm* (2001), in *Kodak*, the full impact of color has migrated indoors to the timeless and artificial lighting of the factory. *Kodak* has only one sequence that shows a window to the outside world, when a worker eats his lunch in the canteen. As in *Gellért*, the factory is a windowless place, with no possibility of registering whether it is night or day. As if to insist on this, in the exhibition of her work at Miami Art Central, Dean hung a red light bulb, evocative of the darkroom, at the entrance of the room where *Kodak* was being shown.

Kodak follows the progress of the production process, rather than that of the technicians, who come and go in a way not dissimilar to people in Dean's other films. Because of the long, static shots, people move in and out of frame, entering and leaving. Likewise, their voices are drowned out by the sound of the machinery, which in turn mingles with the whir of the projector in the room as we watch the film. If anything, we watch their movements in a way indifferent to their human subjectivity—they might as well be the diners and waiters in *Fernsehturm* or the magpies in *Pie*, as if we simply observed the migratory patterns of their movements from a distance. There are also the smaller patterns of movement, the inadvertent gestures, the kinds of movements that, again, are of apparently no consequence and have no particular meaning, the often pointless things we do without knowing that we do them. In turn, this reflects back on the movements of the spectators in the space in front of the image, and the comings and goings in the gallery. And while our own movements may never be entirely unpremeditated, the friction between pattern and chance transforms, however temporarily, our encounter with the work of art and with each other. This, in the end, is exhilarating rather than melancholic.

Dean herself has said that she wants to be "invisible,"[23] and it is true that she does not impose herself on her films. Nonetheless, the films possess a powerful sense of a bodily presence. Whose? It does not matter. Nor does it have to do with whether or not people figure in them. It would be as true of *Bubble House* as of *Gellért*, of *Pie* as of *Fernsehturm*. An almost imperceptible breath of movement seems to be instilled in the celluloid. Because the shots are static, we become even more aware of the tiny micro-movements of film itself, where the film moves through the gate twenty-four times a second, "pulling the film by the sprockets" and creating a barely visible shudder that Dean finds "magical."[24] This makes film feel like a corporeal substance as well as an evanescent one. The coincidence of a mechanical process of filming with a human presence that seems an almost accidental effect of that mechanical process—the two coalescing so entirely in the medium of celluloid—seems to be the driving impulse behind her attachment to analogue film. Rather than a nostalgic longing for a past that has gone, it is the way celluloid registers the materiality of the present that continues to captivate us.

Notes

1 "Thirteen Ways of Looking at a Blackbird," in *The Collected Poems of Wallace Stevens* (New York: Alfred A. Knopf, 1972), p. 92.

2 "Pie," in *Tacita Dean: Selected Writings* (Paris: Musée d'Art moderne de la Ville de Paris/ARC, 2003), n.p.

3 As Mark Godfrey has written, "Dean's texts may anchor the films, but only in the way of one who knows how the power of waves can make anchors slip." See his article, "Time has Told Me," *Frieze* 88 (January/February 2005), p. 104. See also his "Photography Found and Lost: On Tacita Dean's *Floh*," *October* 114 (Fall 2005), pp. 90–119.

4 "Pie," n.p.

5 "The Green Ray," in *Tacita Dean: Selected Writings*, n.p.

6 The title of the present essay is an obvious reference to Sebald's book *On the Natural History of Destruction*, trans. Anthea Bell (New York: Random House, 2003), but also to Robert Smithson's question at the end of his essay of circa 1971, "Art Through the Camera's Eye": "If art history is a nightmare, then what is natural history?" See *Robert Smithson: The Collected Writings*, ed. Jack Flam (Berkeley: University of California Press, 1996), p. 375.

7 "Once Upon a Different Sort of Time, The Story of Donald Crowhurst," in *Tacita Dean: Selected Writings*, n.p. J.G. Ballard has noted that, in her written account, she focuses on Crowhurst's obsession with his chronometer, which, when he loses it, precipitates his fall into madness. See Ballard's "Time and Tacita Dean," in *Tacita Dean* (London: Tate Gallery Publishing Limited, 2001), p. 33.

8 "The *Nautilus* and the Drunken Boat," in *Mythologies*, trans. Annette Lavers (New York: Hill and Wang, 2001), p. 67.

9 Ibid., p. 65.

10 The change occurs between this film and *Disappearance at Sea* (1996). Dean has explained, "There was a shift around *Disappearance at Sea*, which became about leaving the narrative off." See her interview with Roland Groenenboom, in *Tacita Dean* (Milan: Postmedia Books, 2004), n.p.

11 "Sound Mirrors," in *Tacita Dean: Selected Writings*, n.p.

12 in *Tacita Dean: Selected Writings*, n.p.

13 J.G. Ballard, "The Sound-Sweep" (1960), in *The Voices of Time and Other Stories* (New York: Berkeley Medallion, 1962).

14 Robert Smithson, "Incidents of Mirror-Travel in the Yucatan," *Artforum* 8, no. 1 (September 1969); reprinted in *Robert Smithson: The Collected Writings*, p. 129.

15 "Palast," in *Tacita Dean: Selected Writings*, n.p.

16 This has been written about extensively and especially finely by Michael Newman in "Salvage," in *Tacita Dean: Essays* (Paris: Musée d'Art moderne de la Ville de Paris/ARC, 2003), n.p. Newman also invokes something not only lost, but retrieved and saved in the work.

17 See Julia Kristeva, *Black Sun: Depression and Melancholia*, trans. Leon S. Roudiez (New York: Columbia University Press, 1989), p. 25.

18 On this theme of communality, see Newman's discussion of "plural sociality based on talk and bodily pleasures, without excluding the labour needed to create its conditions," in relation to Dean's *Fernsehturm*, in his "Tacita Dean: Fictions du temps qui tourne," in *Les Cahiers du Musée national d'art moderne* no. 86 (January 2004). See also Tamara Trodd's important question in her discussion of Dean and the idea of the medium: "What form of collectivity can be achieved between subjects who imaginatively inhabit different and illusory time-streams?" See her "Film at the End of the Twentieth Century: Obsolescence and the Medium in the Work of Tacita Dean," *Object* (London) no. 6 (2003/2004), p. 52.

19 Tacita Dean, "Analogue," in *Tacita Dean: Analogue, Drawings 1991–2006*, ed. Theodora Vischer and Isabel Friedli, (Basel: Schaulager, and Göttingen: Steidl, 2006), pp. 8–9.

20 "The Green Ray," n.p. The shortest of Dean's films is *Diamond Ring* at 27 seconds.

21 "Sound Mirrors," n.p.

22 Derek Jarman, *Chroma: A Book of Colour—June '93* (London: Century, 1994), p. 145.

23 Dean made this point in a lecture given at the Goethe Institute, London, on 1 February 2007.

24 Dean, in a letter to the author, 16 February 2007.

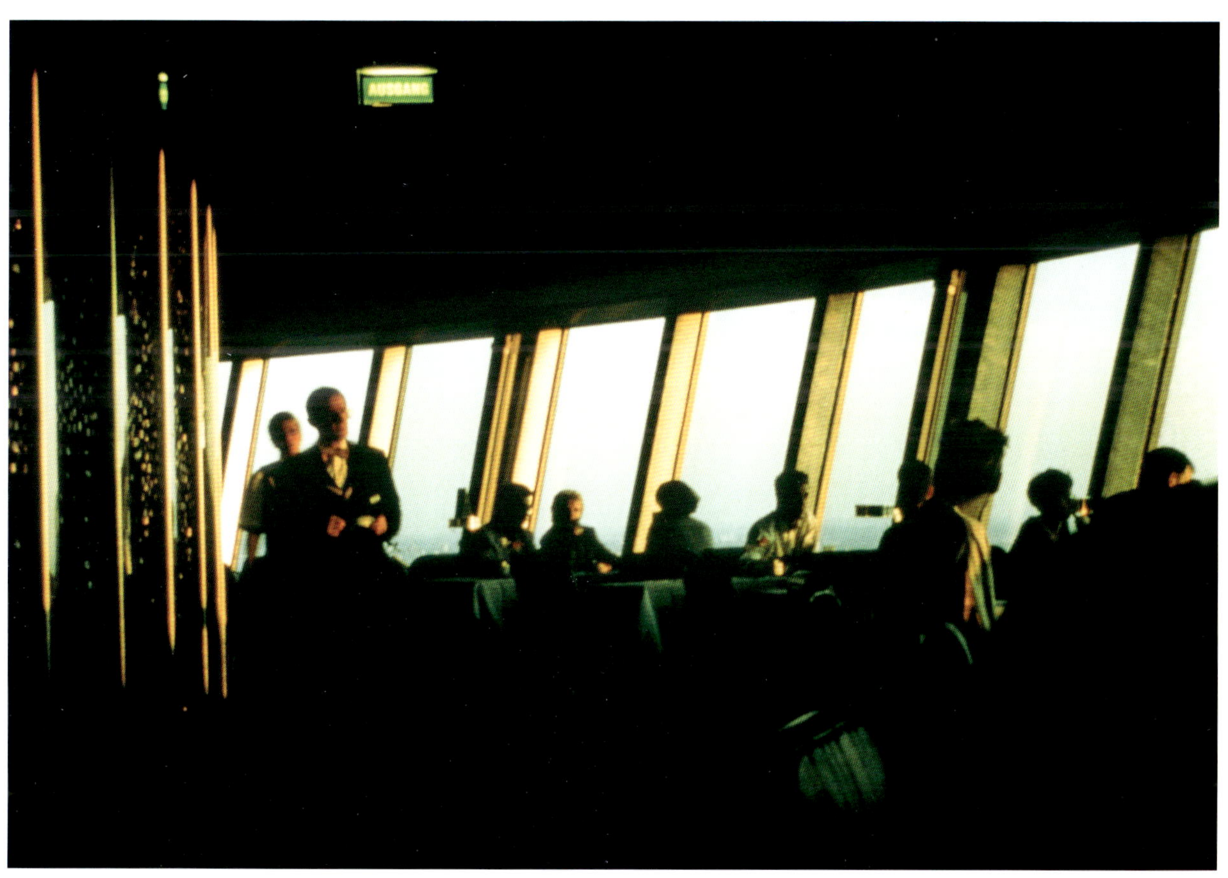

Fernsehturm

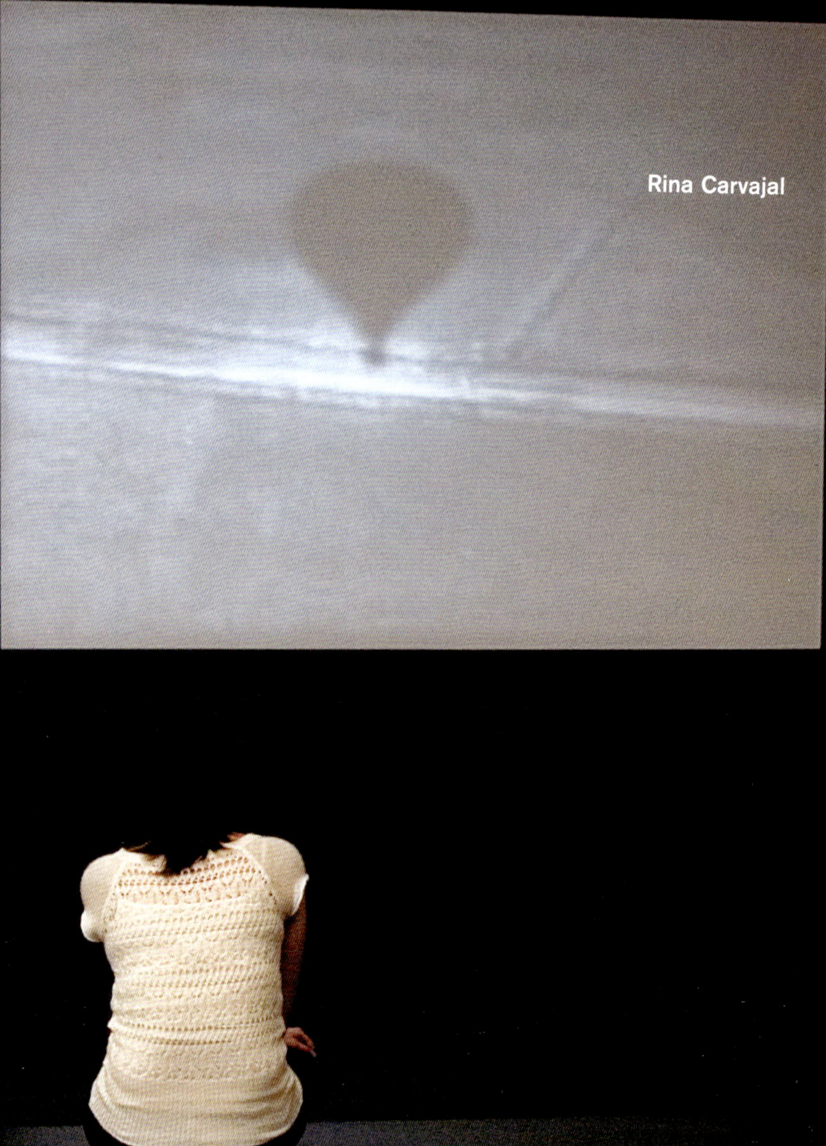

Rina Carvajal

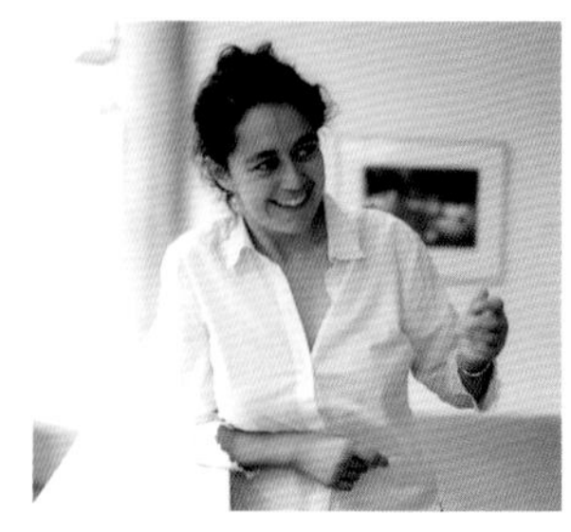

Rina Carvajal: Why is 16mm film, in particular, so attractive to you at a time when digital technology has made film all but obsolete?

Tacita Dean: When I started working with film it wasn't a digital age. But, as of late, it has come and taken us, and me. I am still working with the medium that I found and fell in love with when I was a student. It's just the rapidity with which the digital age has pushed film aside that makes it suddenly look as if I'm working with obsolete technology like a fetishist. But I'm not; I'm just fighting for the medium I love.

RC: Do you think 16mm film will survive?

TD: No, it won't. There are a few things that are important here. A lot of cinematographers are very disillusioned with digital and they always try to work on film. There's no depth of field, there's no black, there's all sorts of problems with digital, but when the generation that remembers film have gone, it will become much more difficult. The world divides into digital natives and digital immigrants. We're digital immigrants; my son will be a digital native. He won't know what a negative is. It's going to disappear. I think it's tragically sad. I think it's altering more than just our image culture, it's altering our culture profoundly. It terrifies me, actually. Also, a lot of people are losing their images, because they are not backing them up, or putting them in the new formats. But if you have a negative, you will always have a negative. You can see a negative that's over a hundred years old now. When I was at college—and I'm not that old—everything was done on U-matic. Do you remember U-matic?

RC: No. What is it?

TD: U-matic video was the early video technology. All the stuff I did as a student on U-matic is practically impossible to transfer off now. Whereas film is solid, it's tangible; it's not about that sort of failing.

RC: Also, the editing is so much more physical and tactile.

TD: It is totally, utterly, and profoundly different from working with digital technology. What staggers me, actually, is how people just don't know the difference. You say, "This is film," and they say, "Well, what is the difference between film and video?" People of my generation and older should really know that, because they grew up with film. They didn't grow up with video. Film is celluloid, and is about light and emulsion and lenses. Digital and video are all about pixelization and electronic code. There's an opacity to it; you can't look at the picture when you hold it up to light. So, it is a battle. I've got a hell of a battle on my hands. I'm already fighting it.

RC: Do you think that film will still be used by a specialized group of people?

TD: Well, artists and some filmmakers are the only people who care about the presentation of images; however, we are too few and not very vociferous. Everyone else gets immediately transformed into another medium. The only people that care about film, really, apart from artists and filmmakers, are archivists. People will remember the aura of film, but nobody else needs to present it. They go on to the medium of television, to the medium of billboards, magazines, and stuff like that. Nobody cares about the end of film, except for visual artists.

I will struggle on to the bitter end with film. The death of film has been announced for a while now and yet it's still quite strong. The real victim of the moment is photography; photographic papers have disappeared. It's terrible. Digital has taken over still photography more rapidly than moving images.

RC: Is sound, or the fiction of sound, important in your work?

TD: Sound is fantastically important in my work. On my way here, I just came from doing the sound for my new film. It starts with a seven-minute sequence of wind in an orchard, and I just worked so hard on trying to get the right emotional pitch for the wind. I realize that I feel utterly confident in sound and the choreography of sound. I've developed a whole system of creating soundtracks for my films. One thing that's very important about film is that it is always recorded silently. It's a mute medium and therefore the soundtrack is its own autonomous thing. Of course, you can have sync sound that's recorded separately, and that's what a clapper is for, so you can recognize visually where you are on the sound.

I use sync sound, but so much of sound in film is something that you fabricate. I don't think people realize that. *Foley Artist* from 1996 was a learning curve for me, when I realized the efficiency of sound. It was a complete creation of a soundtrack. I said I wanted rain and the

Foley artist puts down wet newspaper. And the sound was just so descriptive. In my new film, *Michael Hamburger*, for example, there are periods in which I want there to be rain. I didn't film any rain, but, by using the sound, you are utterly convinced that it's raining. You begin to see the movement of rain in the film because sound is so powerful. I love it. I'm so confident of that when I'm working with sound. With the wind, I just thought, "we can't have any birds, we've got to lose the birds." It has to be very emotional. It's very intuitive, and yet it's something I completely love doing.

I also use sound in relation to memory. I might put in dogs barking that are not there as a very telling of a description of a moment in time. Because the films are all about the very simple depiction of a moment, but I use things from my own autobiography. A motorbike in the distance is, for me, very redolent of a summer evening in my childhood in rural Kent; that sort of sound is so evocative of a certain time of day, of a certain period in time, an emotional relationship to place.

RC: So for you sound triggers these things?

TD: No, but it makes you realize how memory is both entirely personal and universal. I've always been attracted to things that don't function very well in their own time, and that are awkward and strangely gauche in the landscape. I notice them, but why I notice them, why I'm attracted, are the things that are too difficult for me on earth. But I do like these places and people, and I like to try to depict them in time. Film is a medium of time. That's why I could never swap to a more "efficient" medium. Digital is an efficient medium, but it's not about time at all. It's not about anything that I care about, actually. I don't think people realize the specificity of film. I'm very upset about its sudden demise—the year and a half I've had to become more upset about it, because it's so quick.

RC: Your earlier films like *The Martyrdom of St. Agatha* (1994), *The Story of Beard* (1992), and *A Bag of Air* (1995) have important narrative dimensions. They involved fictional stories and voiceover narrations that are absent in subsequent films. More recently, narrative has returned to some of your films. Could you tell me about this?

TD: The film that marked the change was *Disappearance at Sea* in 1996.

I was working with the story of Donald Crowhurst and thinking about how lighthouses were human beacons on the edge of the immensity of the ocean. It was a project for a lighthouse and I was filming lighthouses. I went to two lighthouses, one north of Berwick-upon-Tweed, one south; one was in Scotland, one in England. The one in Scotland was a lighthouse that had only the head. It was set in to the cliff; there was no tower. So I could actually be at the beacon head, looking in. And suddenly it was visually exhilarating. I expected to be standing with my back to the lighthouse, looking out to the sea, and I turned around and looked into the bulbs of the lighthouse. It became a film about the lighthouse, but the footage was so stunning when I got it back that it took my breath away. I collected the sound, which is the sound of the turning of the lighthouse, but also the birds getting more and more hysterical. It wasn't chronological in the same sense that it is in my film—how it builds up to a crescendo—which is what I did to it to make it more emotional. And there was no room for my voiceover. It was a turning point, not only in terms of that film and the jettisoning of the voiceover, which I went back to in *The Structure of Ice* a year after *Disappearance at Sea*. So, I did go back to the voiceover but that has been my last. And it was a complete liberation.

Disappearance at Sea

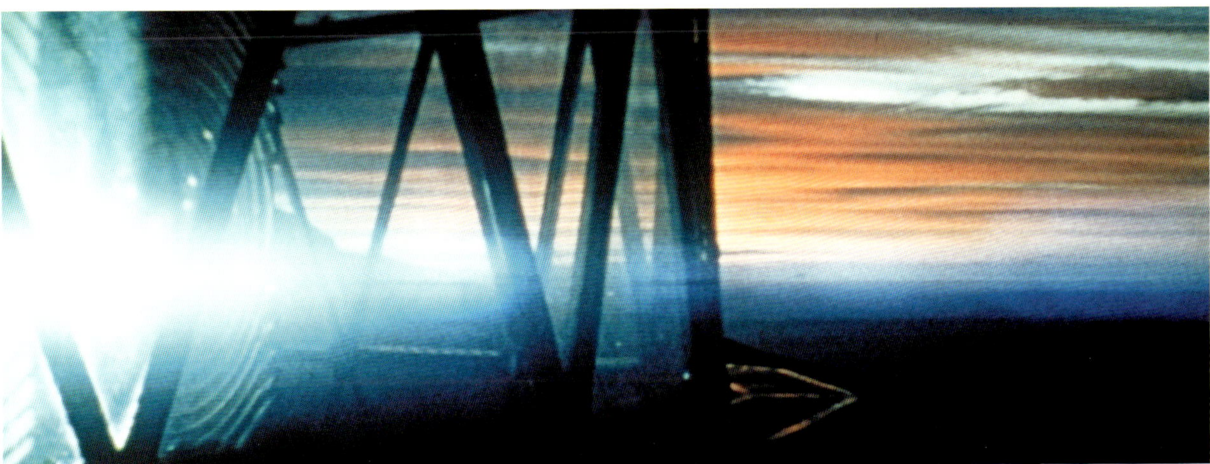

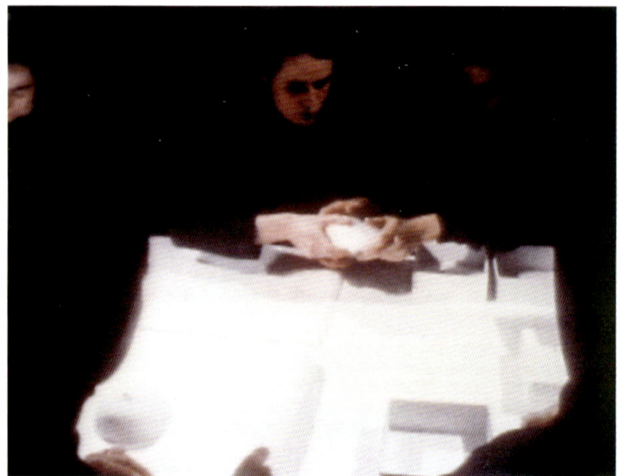

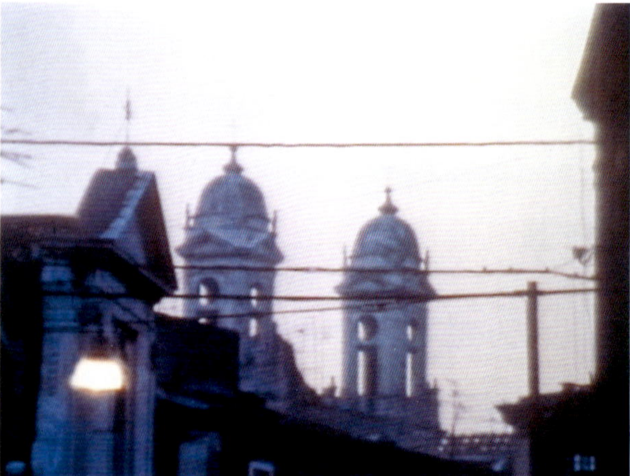

The Matyrdom of St. Agatha

That was also the year I went to Sundance, and what was extraordinary about that is that, within the art world in Britain, *The Martyrdom of St. Agatha* was a detested and loathed work. People hated being trapped by that degree of narrative, even though it was a fictional narrative. *Disappearance at Sea* was my first truly sculptural work, much more related to sculptural and painterly traditions than *Agatha*, which was a narrative work. But when I went to Sundance, it was the total opposite. They all loved *The Martyrdom of St. Agatha* and they just did not understand *Disappearance at Sea*. It was a complete watershed for me. I understood more about reception and context, and, at that point, the narrative went into my writing and it left the artwork alone.

RC: Is that why you ended up choosing to show your work in specialized art spaces?

TD: It was not that I was choosing to make it for the art world, it was that I was finding my own language. I didn't need this dependency on narrative; I could liberate myself from the narrative. I'd had an epiphany with *The Story of Beard* when I was a student in 1992. I had all this information about hair, and the history of hair, and history of beards, and I'd just film all these little cameo things, and at a certain point I just sat down and I wrote the narrative, the voiceover for *The Story of Beard*. And suddenly I realized I could take all that factual information and wade through it by creating fiction, and that was liberating. The voice-over enabled me to tell a whole story from all this intense research I'd done. And then *Disappearance at Sea* showed me a way to have all that, but not have to rely on the fiction so much. Now my films have changed even more. They're changing the whole time. I don't even know how they are going to change, but the longer films with people in them are becoming slightly more narrative.

RC: Why do you present your films in varying formats?

TD: Each one has very much to do with the nature of the film. The anamorphic format, for instance, widens; I have double the amount of picture frame.

Initially, I showed the 1999 film *Banewl* way too big and realized that such a physically dark film has to be like a little intense jewel, with perfect conditions and very good sound, so that you forget your body. It's all about waiting, waiting for this cosmic event, and then the anticlimax, as well as the climax. And *Kodak* was also very visceral. I wanted it to be reminiscent of watching film in a lab. My intuition was that its installation had to have no objects in the room, so the projector had to be fixed to the back of the wall. With *The Green Ray*, from 2001, you have to bear witness to the beginning, so it had to operate on a push button. Working in this way, I'm more of a visual artist than a filmmaker.

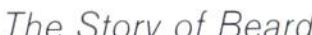

The Story of Beard

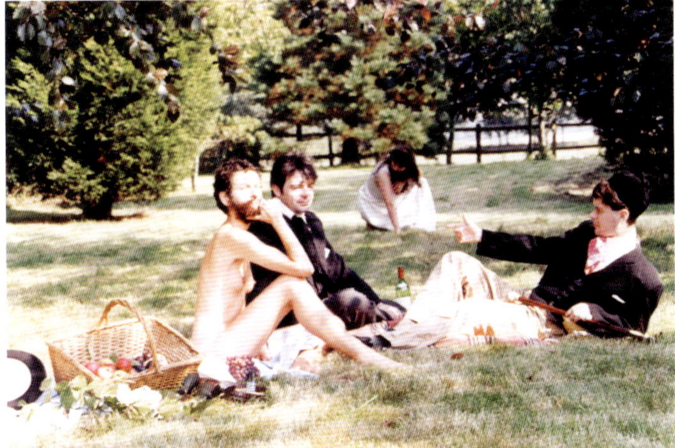

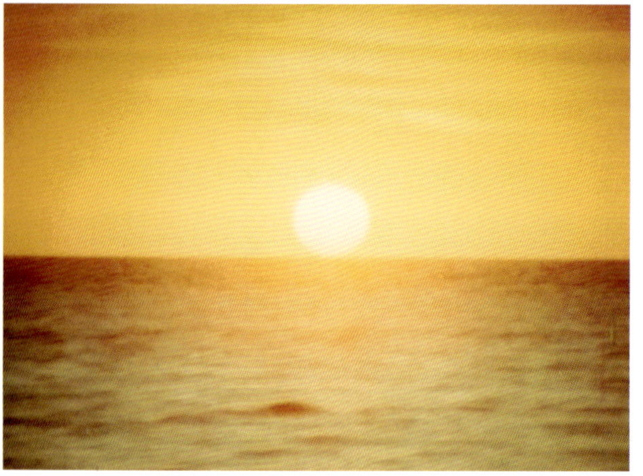
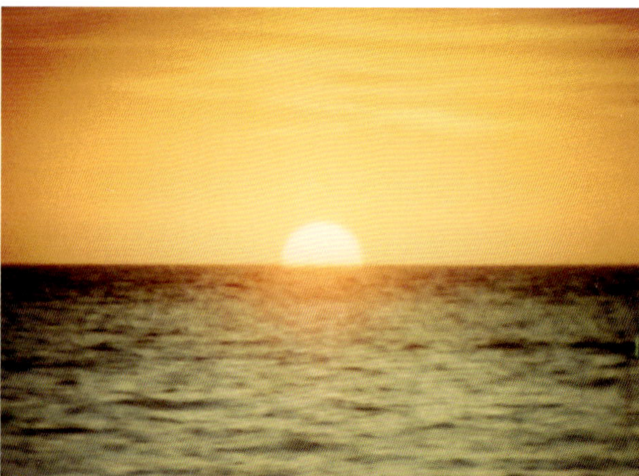

The Green Ray

I refuse to have my films shown in cinemas because they're just inappropriate and wrong. They are works for galleries. *The Uncles*, from 2004, is the only film I've actually made for a cinema. I used anamorphic for that because I wanted to have both the uncles sitting really large and comfortably in the frame. At normal format, I would have had just room for one of them.

RC: What about *Boots* (2003) and the fact that it is installed in three rooms?

TD: *Boots* depends entirely upon how it's installed. It's basically three languages. People think it's the same film in three languages, but it's actually three entirely different films. Boots becomes three different people, not consciously, but when he spoke a different language he changed; there is a metamorphosis. I realized after exhibiting the work at Schaulager in Basel in 2006 that to show it in any other way—which I've had to do because there is never enough room—is wrong for the work, because it's so great to have the partial view of all three.

Boots was British, spent his childhood in Germany, and lived in France. He was a polyglot of that period in time; a 1930s cosmopolitan European, he could speak three languages. At a certain point during the filming, I asked, "Would you say something?" I was too chaotic to have organized that in advance. When I was editing—because every-

thing happens in editing—I thought, this is it. I have to make one in German, one in English, and one in French. Then I decided to designate different rooms. It meant I'd lose a lot of good footage, because he'd spoken three languages in each room. So in English, he's in one room; in German, he's in another. But the French, for which I chose the dining room, was a bit like Pluto. He said one word in the French room. I gave myself a hurdle that was almost impossible to climb over, but it was a discipline, a format that I had to adhere to. That's how the format came, through the editing. I hadn't been organized enough to think about that before. I never am. I never am. I'm very chaotic in the filming stage, actually.

RC: Several of your films try to capture the unfolding of natural events in real time. In *Banewl, Totality* (2000), and *Diamond Ring* (2002), for example, you try to capture the imperceptible motion of a solar eclipse, and in *The Green Ray*, the slow setting of the sun until the very last ray fades. *Fernsehturm* (2001), on the other hand, traces a cycle that goes from day to night. What moves you to try to capture a lived experience of time?

TD: *Banewl* was probably the first film that was about a total eclipse of the sun. I didn't know what to expect at all. My ambition was originally to make a two-hour and forty-four-minute film, which is the entire length

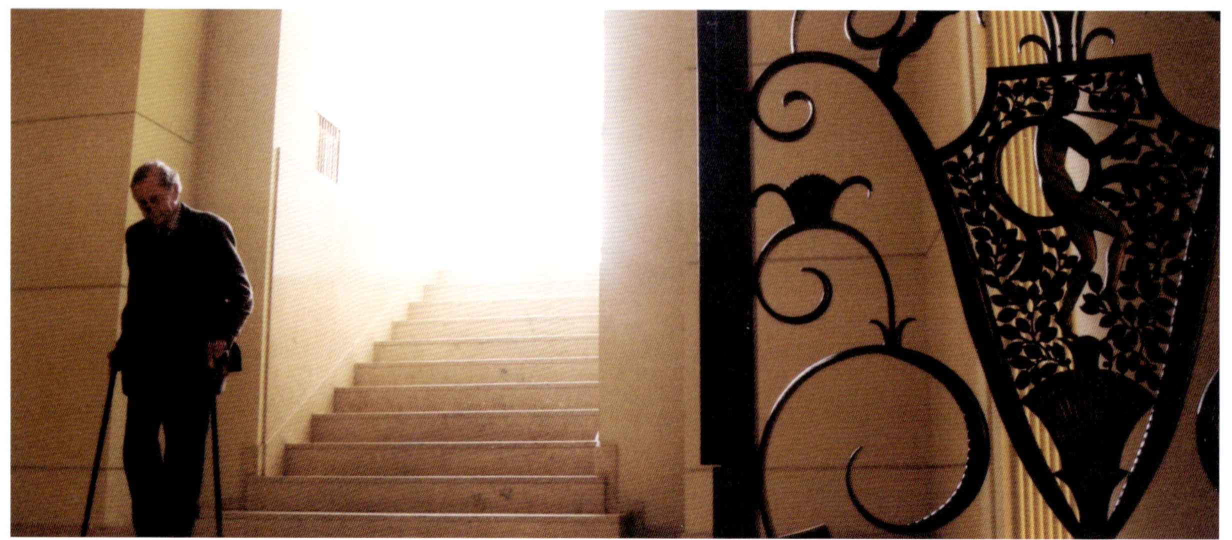

Boots

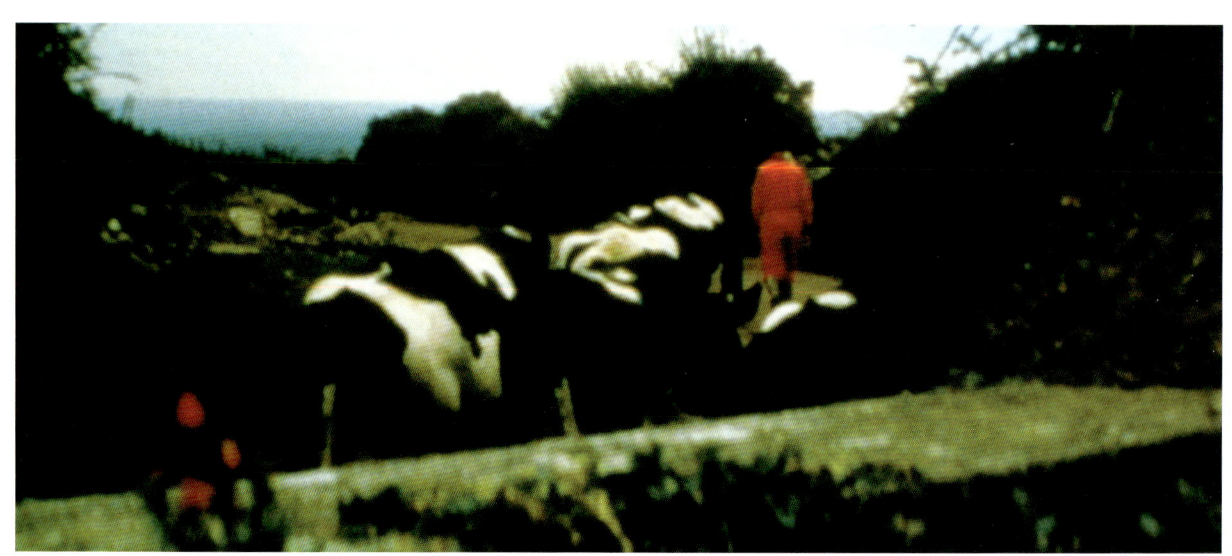

Banewl

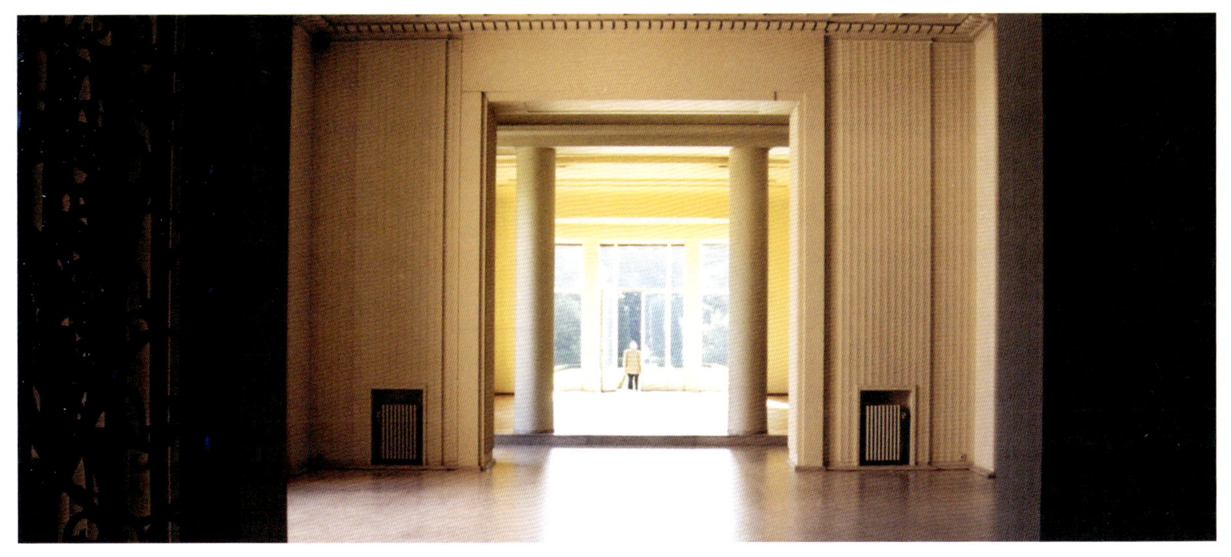

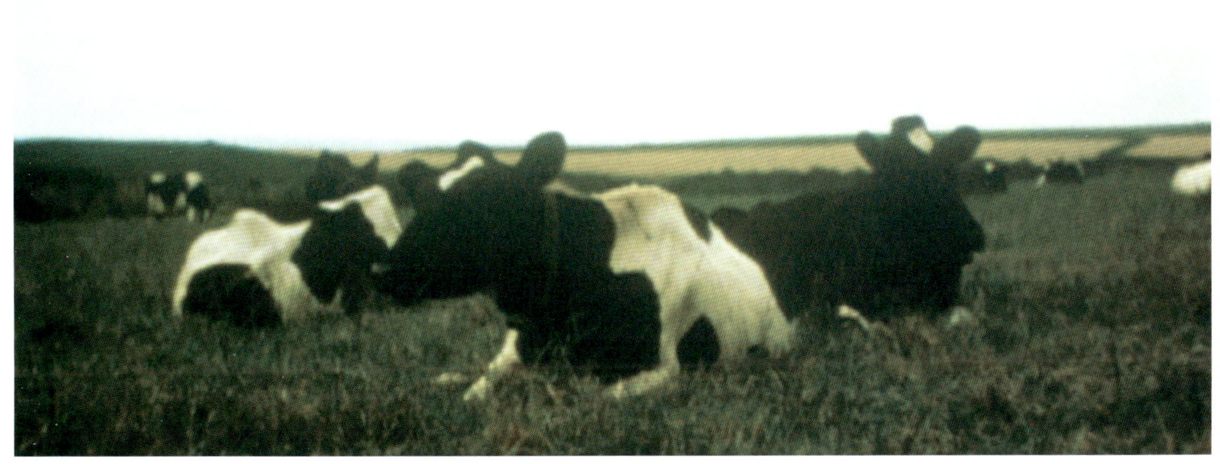

of the eclipse. I had four cameras and everyone was choreographed so that there wasn't going to be any missing time. It was incredibly intense. And then it started to rain, there was no sign of any action in the sky at all, one camera jammed up, and, at a certain point—I was on a dairy farm in Cornwall—I realized that I couldn't possibly make this a real-time film and I had to do something quite other. We had walkie-talkies, and they kept saying, "Well, do we bother filming, do we bother filming?" I kept saying, "Yes, you've got to film, you have to film, it's really important." But they didn't film with the same intensity as if the eclipse had been visible. And so, at a certain point, I said, we've got a film not of the sky but the ground. This film is going to be about the changes on the ground. So, I made the film very, very deliberately boring.

Banewl is sixty-three minutes. It's this very slow waiting for the totality, which is an overcast totality, but it's incredibly dramatic. And I was on a dairy farm, so the cows lay down, the swallows went crazy. It was in August, and it was supposed to be warm, but it had been raining and then it became overcast, and I just filled in the tiny details of the natural world and how the animals reacted. They knew it was coming before we humans did. And when it comes, the actual totality is incredible because, just by chance—and this is really one of those gifts—it was eleven minutes long; the actual totality was one whole roll of film. The cows sit down and the eclipse comes over like an incredible darkness, but you still have this glow, a kind of yellow glow on the horizon, and then this lighthouse came on automatically. Then light comes back and it's a totally different light. It's transformative, a pearly, translucent light. I could never have imagined these things because I had no idea.

RC: Did the other films with eclipses come from the experience of *Banewl*?

TD: Yes and no. They did, because one of the four cameras used for *Banewl* filmed the sky, and that camera's film then became *Totality*. After that, I had a rabid desire to see a real eclipse, so I went two years later to Madagascar. There, it was just me and my little camera, so I only had two and a half minutes per roll. When it came to totality, I was with my American friend Dick and he realized at that moment, which he had waited for longer, probably, than me, that he hadn't got any film in his camera. So he had this comical moment, because, of course, it's only a matter of seconds. He said, "I've got no film in my camera," so I gave him my still camera, and while doing it, I clonked the tripod that held my 16mm camera, which just fell down. It was a moment of paralysis, and, at a certain point, I just straightened it and did this very ungainly zoom onto the sun, just as the moon moved over it. In the end, I made *Diamond Ring*, which uses a section of film only twenty-seven seconds long. It's just this clumsy trying to find the sun, and the moment I stop, the moon passes and exposes the film. I made twelve separate negatives and put them all together so that it's a six-and-a-half-minute film, in fact, and twelve is the number of months and all sorts of things.

RC: Time feels very physical in your work. Your films seem to challenge our perception of time, either by the choice of subject matter, the use of the medium, or the way they engage the viewer—slowing down time with long takes and inducing viewers to experience a notion of time framed by their own subjectivity.

TD: Slowing down time for me is also about the fact that time has been very sped up. The time I use is the time of film; it is film time, daring to hold the shot longer than some people find tolerable. I do it less now; my shots are getting shorter.

But it also has so much to do with the way in which I make my

Diamond Ring

films: cutting on a Steenbeck, continually going to and fro and to and fro, and the whole ritual of manufacture. I'm like an artisan in a way. But also, film is the very physical manifestation of time: twenty-four frames a second. If you are working with this physical stuff, you're dealing with physical time, not something that's obtuse and nonlinear, or a screen where you can pluck anything and put it wherever you like. It's really a ritual of time, making a film on a flat table. My films have that, that's just about their manufacture, but within them I use that ritual of time. And it's about my own time, somehow. I'm not imposing a conceptual thing. I actually watch the shot until I think it's time to change it. There's no other rule to it. I don't count, I don't do anything.
I just think it's an intuitive pace. It all slows time because everyone is much more used to a rapid edit of time. And film is about time from the very first moment. You have a spool and it's either two and a half minutes or it's ten minutes, but it's already a pocket of time and you have to make decisions about that in relation to time. It's not a passive thing that has a bit of eternity about it, that just observes; it's all about looking. You have to make decisions about light, about focusing, about sound; you make decisions about everything. It's entirely decisive and entirely about time. That's profound and that's why film is so different from digital technology. It's a language of time and it's all about the editing. I edit in order to create the illusion that time is a continuum. I'm quite formal. I'm a very formal editor.

I care about things. I care about the tiny details of time. For my new film, it's actually been very stressful because I had two cameras filming Michael Hamburger at certain points, and one of the cameramen had the other camera in shot for the whole time. So I get the film back, and it's unusable, because I'm also very formal. I'm not into showing how I made it, which some other people would be. So I had to basically cut from one camera.

RC: Your films are very painterly. They also seem quite aware of a wealth of images from art history. Is reference to a tradition of art important to you?

TD: I started by making *The Martyrdom of St. Agatha* and triptychs based on Tiepolo, but that was a very conscious thing. Later, it was less

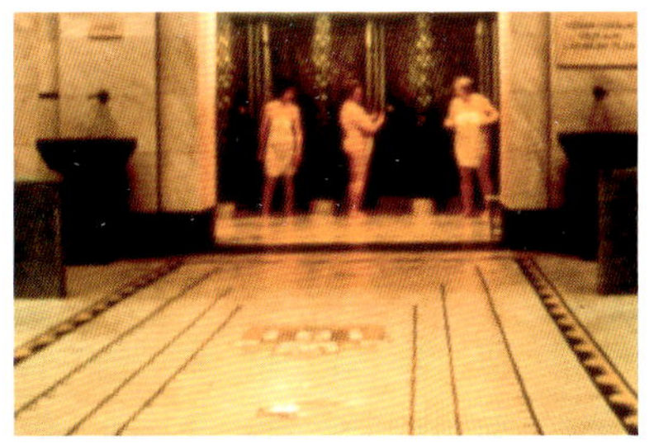
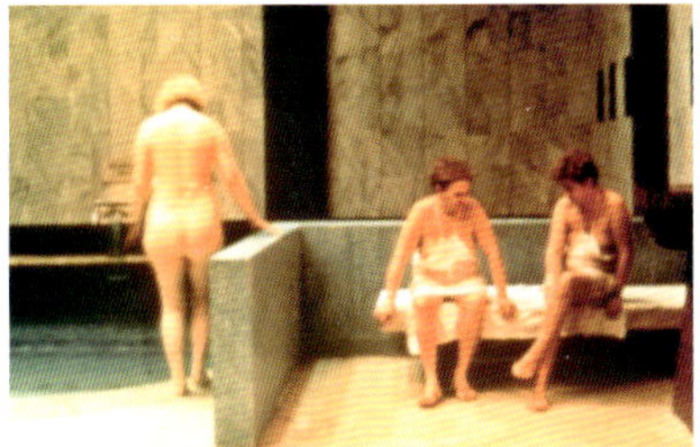
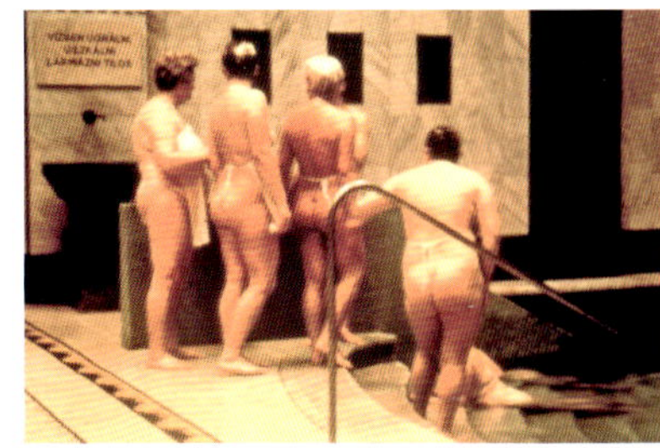

Gellért, 1996, Lamda prints, 15 x 7 1/2 inches

conscious and became a "post-imagined" thing. *Gellért*, from 1998, for example, is pictorial in that sense, but at a certain point I suddenly realized that it was something I'd been trying to find, unconsciously, for a very long time. Do you know the painting by Lucas Cranach the Elder, *The Fountain of Youth*, where these elderly, frail female bodies go in to a pool and come out as nymphs? I loved this painting, and I've had a postcard of it in my life for a very, very long time. I think I just found it in a shop once and I bought it and it's always been there.

I show *Gellért* rear-projected, because it is very much connected with the painted image. The same is true for *Pie*, from 2003. *Pie* also just happened by chance. I filmed it one night, because the magpies used to come every night to my studio window when I was cutting *Boots*. One night, I opened the window, and it was freezing in Berlin, but they all came that night, because sometimes they're fickle, these birds. But they were totally sweet to me. And the warmth from my studio window combined with the cold air outside, and I didn't know that until I got the footage back. I couldn't understand why it was wobbling. Have you seen it? It's like the whole screen is moving, because of the air, but it became so much like a tapestry. It's like some kind of device, but it was an accident, obviously. There is a sort of flatness to *Pie* that's a bit like *Gellért*, making it very painterly.

In *Palast*, from 2004, I actually thought about Stan Brakhage's *The Text of Light*, when he films an ashtray in detail. I wanted to film with that degree of concentration. Of course, I did nothing like Brakhage in that sense, but the surface of the building was just so extraordinarily attractive. The building is gone now; they've knocked it down. It's a carcass at the moment and I can barely bear to drive past it.

RC: Your work acknowledges finitude. People and objects that are about to disappear are recurring motifs in your films, which often seem premised upon the idea of the vanished or the outmoded.

TD: It took me a long time to realize that that's what I'm interested in, because when I was doing all those earlier things I didn't have a conscious trajectory at all. After my 1999 show *Banewl* opened, Jonathan Jones wrote a review in *The Guardian* that said that my work was about disappearance. I had never thought about it that way, but it was true. Now, of course, I have to think about it, not only in terms of objects, but even more in terms of people. I have ended up filming people because I want to trap something of them on this earth before things change. This first crystallized when I had the opportunity to film Mario Merz in San Gimignano in 2002. I was really grateful, because he died suddenly quite soon afterward and I had managed to not miss the occasion. I think Mario courted it slightly. He was definitely aware of what was happening and wanted to present himself in his physicality more than he had ever done—how he had performed in front of a camera before—which had always been very forthright and dogmatic. But for me, he really wanted to be just physical, his physical self, which was quite amazing. And then it happened again in *Boots* and in other works. I suppose these people are more conscious of their mortality than I have been; they all have been more or less old.

The Uncles had very much to do with recording something that I've lived with my whole life. Basically, *The Uncles* is a film about my two uncles in conversation about their fathers. One of them is my father's brother and one is my uncle through marriage. What had happened was that two men, both pioneers of early British cinema, each had a son that had married one of a pair of sisters, one of them being my mother and one of them being, obviously, my aunt. And so the two men and their families got united, even though there was a lot of animosity between them. At a certain point, I realized that I hadn't made a document, that a document about this relationship didn't exist. So I made this film, bringing two of the sons, my uncles, together, and they just talked about their fathers and this relationship around Ealing Studios,

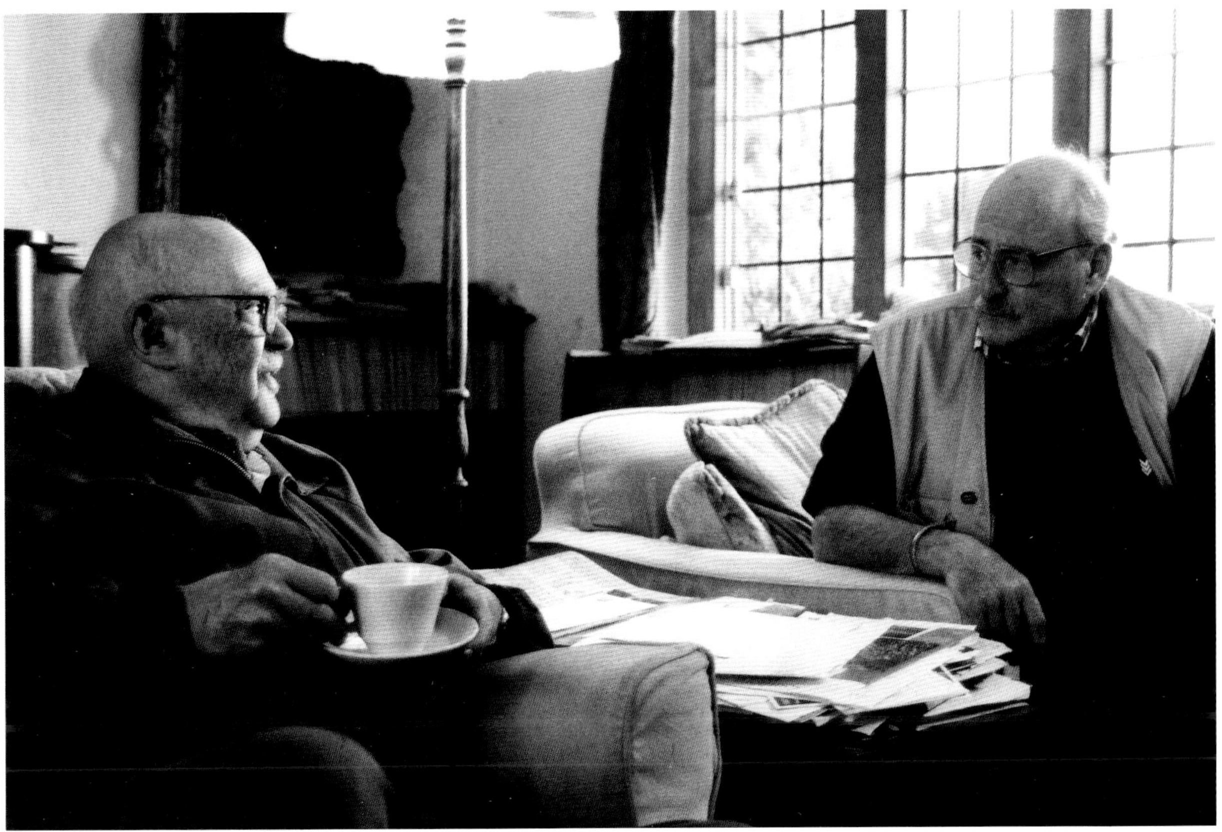

The Uncles

just to explain what that was about. I was very conscious that that story would disappear. That was a piece of oral history more than anything.

RC: Are your films triggers for memory, of stories, people, and things that have been forgotten?

TD: For me, my work is always about the present.

RC: But there always seems to be something in it that harks back to the past, something that recovers or preserves in time people, things, and even film itself, keeping them from disappearing.

TD: I don't want to become too self-conscious about what I do and why I do it. Often the subjects I've chosen are doomed by time, or were doomed, in the case of *Teignmouth Electron*, from 2000, for other reasons. I think it's all very complex and tied up with memory. People have an ambiguous, ambivalent relationship to memory, anyway. So, when you say that it's about recovery, it is difficult for me to really pin that down. Maybe it comes more from the fact that I care about the beauty of an object, and there's recovery within that. It's not like I take a sad old building and make it alive, because I don't do that in any conscious way at all. *A Bag of Air*, for instance, is obviously a film about transformation and healing. And *Kodak*, which is at the other end of it—one was 1995 and the other 2006—becomes elegiac because it is about the beauty of this substance of film and the beauty of the process of creating this substance. It's this beauty that keeps it from being a truly depressing film, I think.

RC: But you do, then, keep these things from completely disappearing.

TD: Only to leave them to die ultimately, anyway. My films are like a suspension of that. I'd probably use a word like "elegiac." People say that my films are often about memory, but memory is such a subjective thing.

Teignmouth Electron, Cayman Brac, 2000, black-and-white photograph >

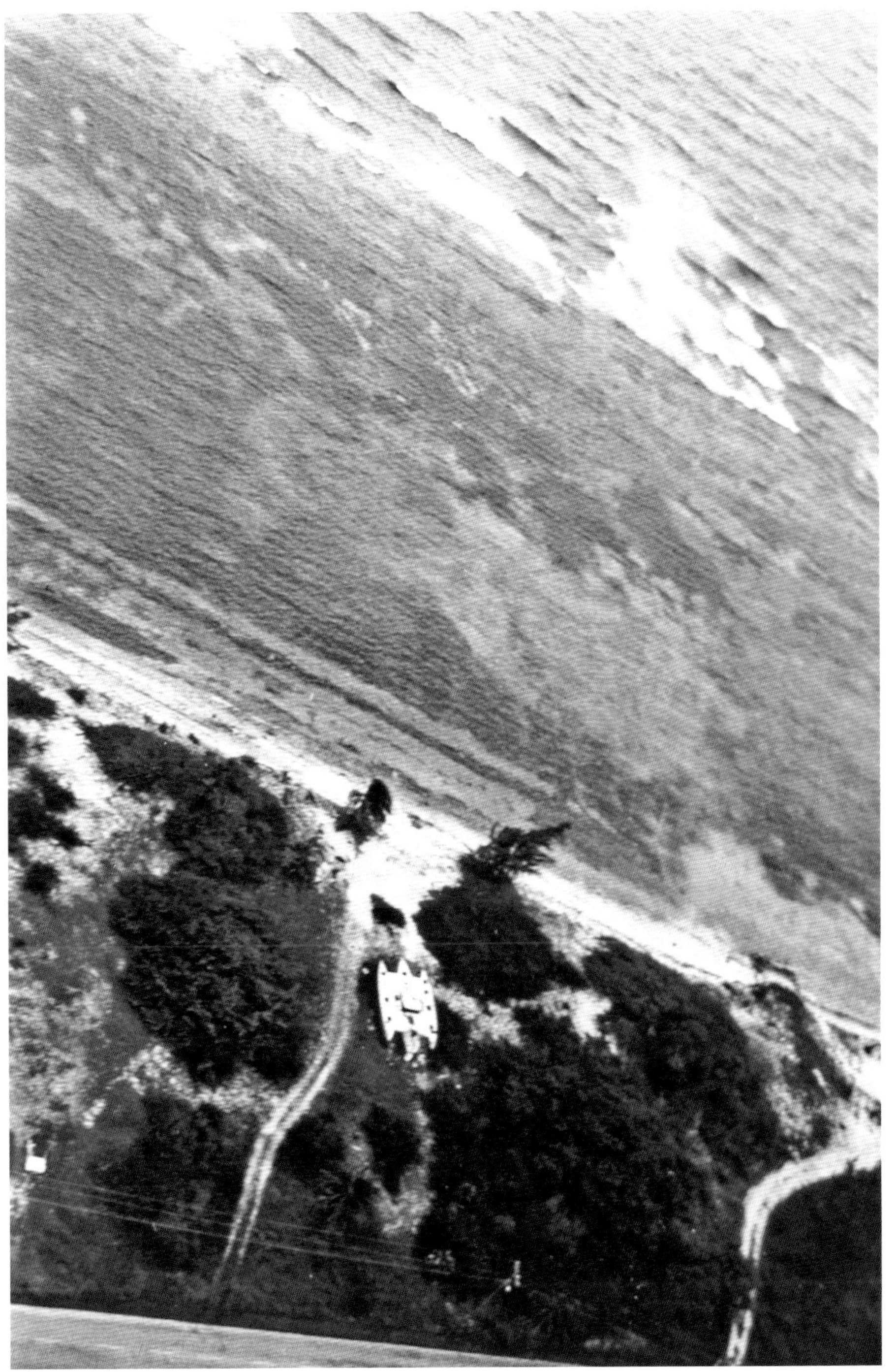

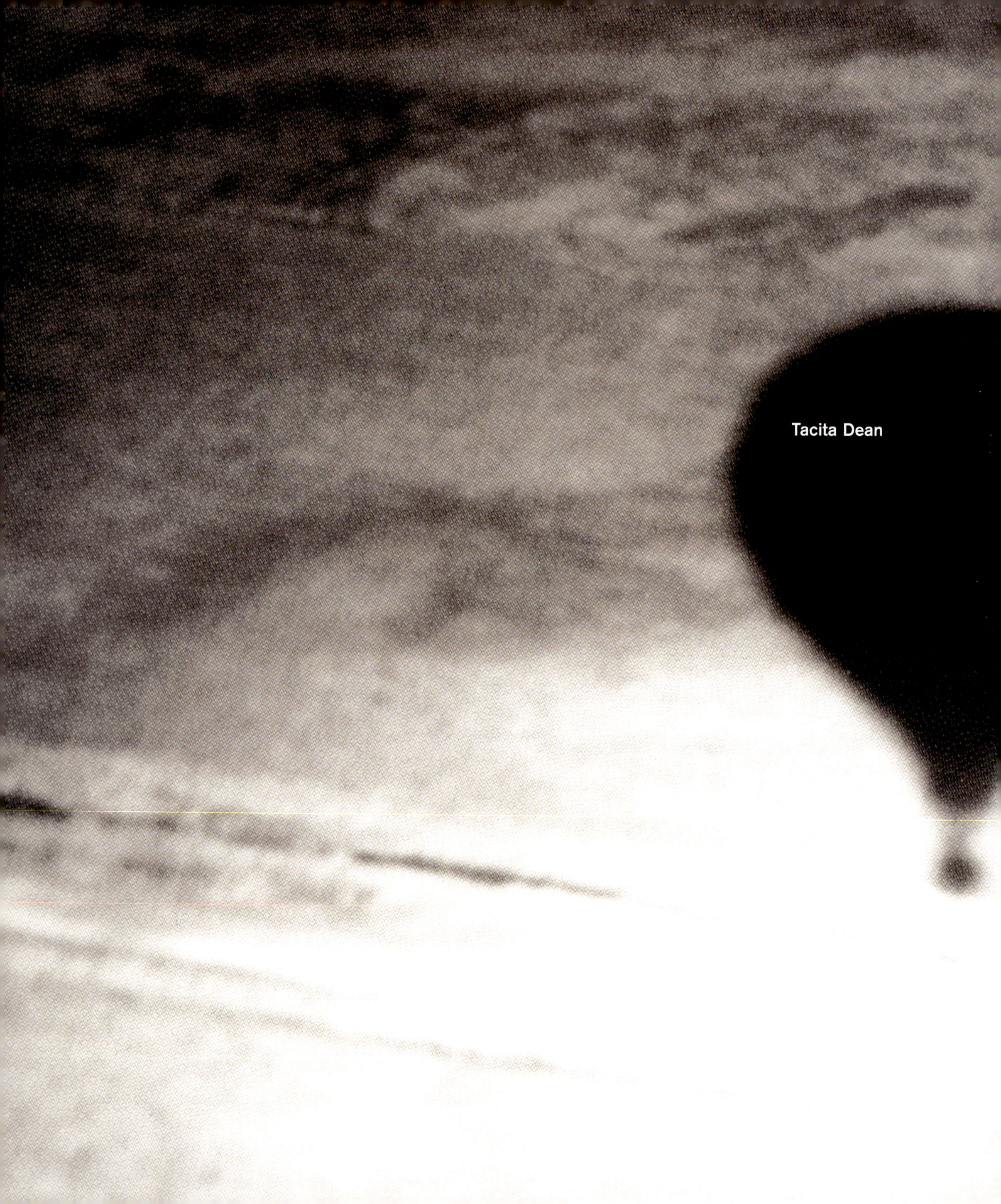
Tacita Dean

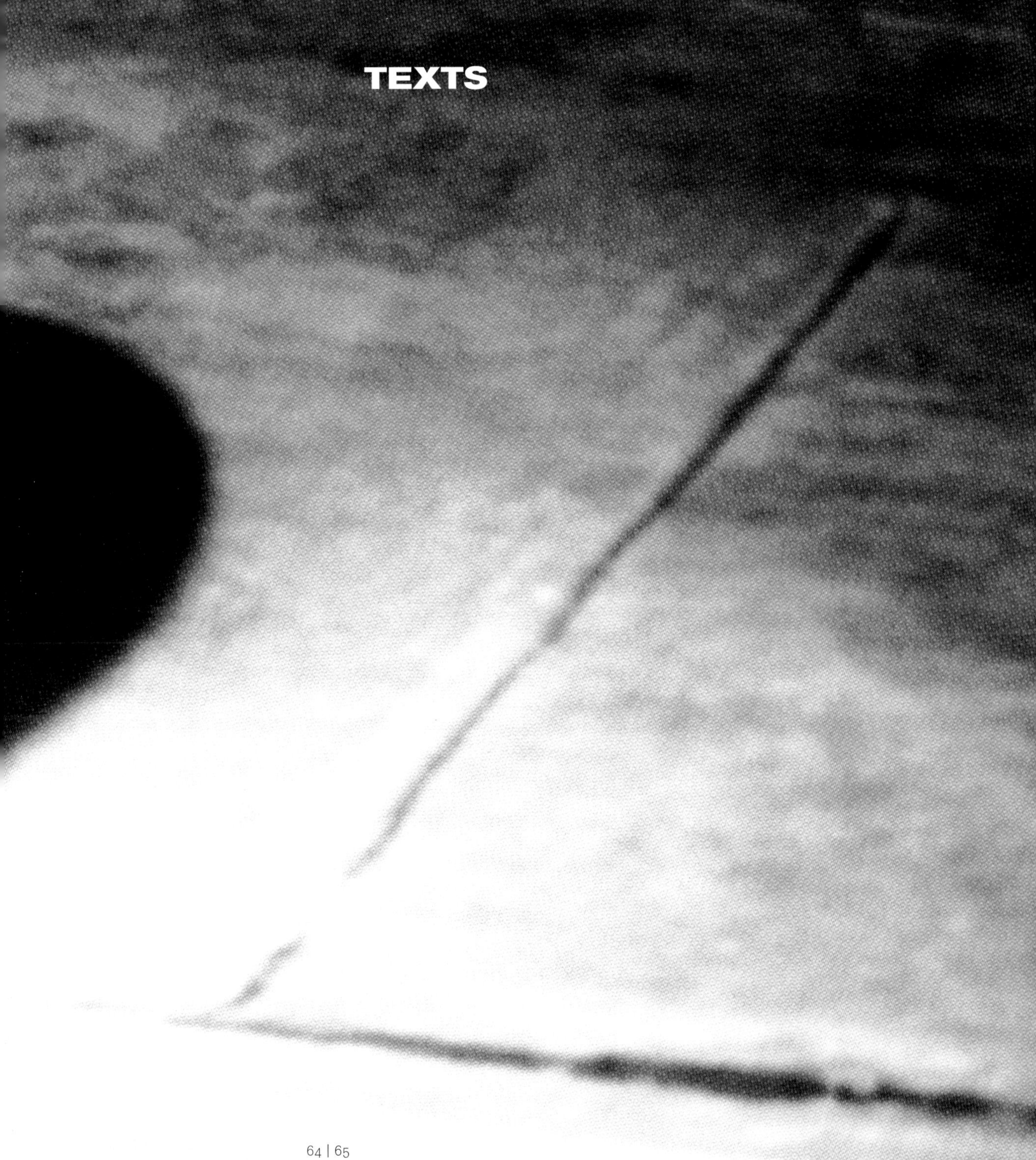

TEXTS

A Bag of Air

If you rise at dawn in a clear sky, and during the month of March, they say you can catch a bag of air so intoxicated with the essence of spring that, when it is distilled and prepared, it will produce an oil of gold, remedy enough to heal all ailments.

And as you rise at dawn to the upper ether, and lean out to catch the bag of air, they say that you are trapping the ascending dew on its voyage from Earth to Heaven. And if you repeat this process each clear dawn for a thousand mornings, you will gather enough essence to fill a sealed flask and to begin your manufacture.

And in your flask will be a delicacy of substance that is both celestial and terrestrial. And if you separate the distillate from the residue each time and over many months, and until you reunite them at the end of your manufacture, they say you will have transformed your bag of air into a golden elixir, a preparation of Etheric medicine capable of treating all disharmonies in the body and soul.

Disappearance at Sea

Berwick lighthouse sits at the end of the quay. The quay stretches out far beyond the town and far beyond the harbor into the water. As the train curls its way around the coast on its approach into Berwick-upon-Tweed, you can fix your eyes upon the dot at the end of the quay that is Berwick lighthouse and imagine the smallness of that enclosed space in relation to the vast immensity of the space beyond: the space that is the sea.

The lighthouse is the last human outpost between land and ocean, and built around human scale. Nonetheless, its presence hints at the otherworldliness of the sea: a different sense of space that will never be domesticated by humankind, and that is more akin to Crowhurst's final and distorted sense of things.

At night, you watch in the blackness for the rotations of the lighthouse and you decipher time in the gaps between the flashes. Without this cipher, there is no time. Crowhurst's "time-madness," where he believed he was floating through prehistory, utterly alone in an unforgiving seascape so far removed from human contact, is only just possible to imagine standing in the last human place where the ocean starts and the land ends in a solitary beacon of safety.

Looming in the window of the lighthouse, where normally the light would be, you can just make out the anguished face of Donald Crowhurst. Like the man in the moon, he becomes the light of the lighthouse, his gaze fixed eternally on the horizon as he looks out upon the sea.

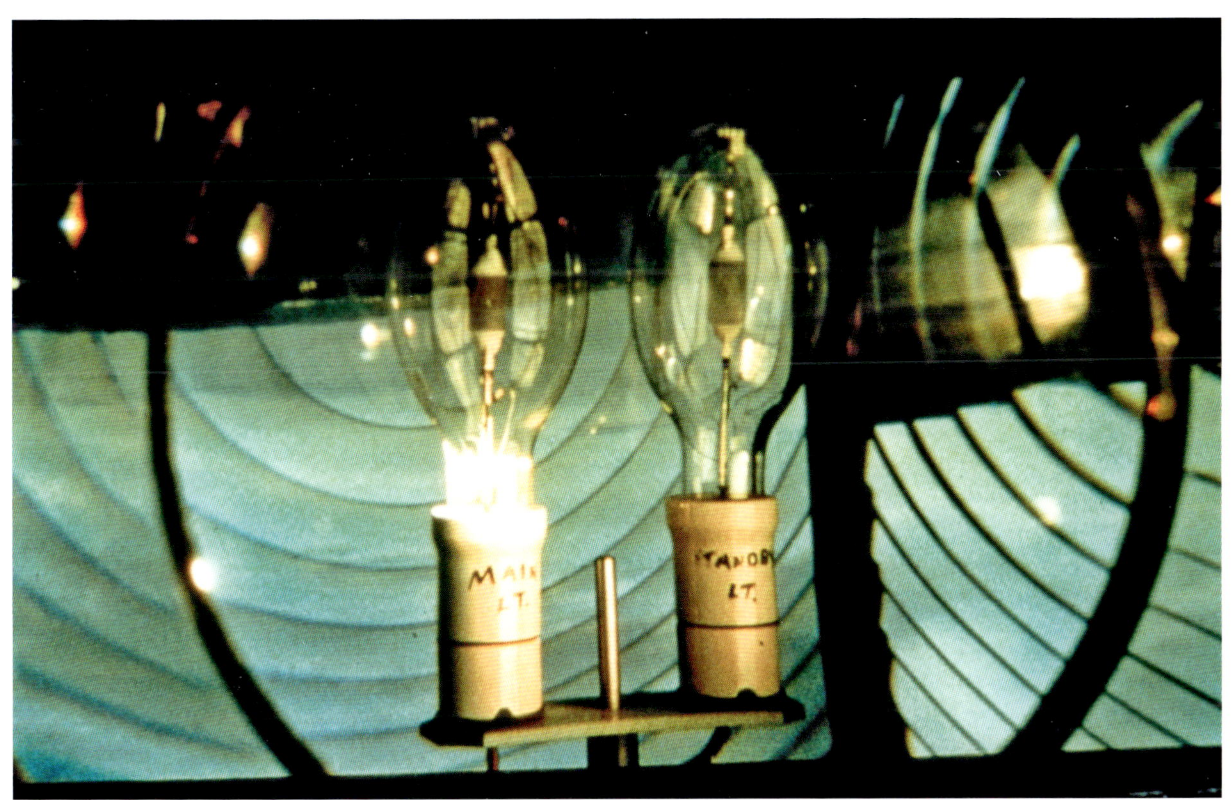

Once Upon a Different Sort of Time: The Story of Donald Crowhurst

The Postcard

In 1968, Donald Crowhurst was one of nine competitors who entered *The Sunday Times* Golden Globe Race to be the first to circumnavigate solo non-stop around the world. He was a family man with a failing business and no professional sailing experience, but his determination to enter and to win, set him on a path of delusion that swept up others and trapped him into leaving in an unfit boat, ill prepared and afraid. Crowhurst's story is as much about his bravado and the politics of a small provincial town as it is about epic voyages and heroism.

When you catch what used to be called the *Cornish Riviera* to Penzance, you pass through a stretch of Devon where the cliff has broken away to form stacks along the coast, and the railway track borders on the sea. The train never stops at the station there, and is often moving too fast for you to make out its name. I was always fascinated by the thought of this place and I at last found myself there, because this was Teignmouth, the town where Crowhurst set out from, and his intended home port for the race.

I was looking for a postcard that I was sure had been produced to commemorate the event. I wanted some physical proof of the story: a token that would connect the man to the place. We went first to a newsagent but they had never heard of him and told us to try the docks. We wandered to a concrete jetty where a group of men were loading sand onto a trawler. I tapped the glass and asked a man in the security box. He told me to try Fred Tooley, who used to be on the Council. Fred Tooley was sitting in the dockers' cafe. He remembered Crowhurst very well and thought he did have a couple of those postcards somewhere. If he could find them, and did have two, he'd let me have one. We arranged to meet him later in a pub on the front where he was working as a bouncer.

We walked up to the Council offices: a house set in a park on the hill that looked out to sea. We had to start thinking about spending the night in Teignmouth and here were a row of bed-and-breakfasts that afforded a view of the docks.

Crowhurst's voyage was inextricably caught up with the affairs of Teignmouth Council. He became a tool for their Publicity Committee and, after he had found financial support for the construction of his trimaran locally, he named it *Teignmouth Electron* after the town. From what I can gather, he probably loved being the darling of Teignmouth in those few hectic months prior to his departure, but gradually this local pride became too much to bear and, in those agonising days when he was desperately trying to get ready to leave, he must have despised the bunting on the quay and the dignitaries preparing to wave him off. They stood between him and his way of escape. He must have known there was no getting out of it then, and that he was trapped by his own bravado and by their zealous civic pride.

I had been particularly struck by the closing paragraph in the book written on Crowhurst by the two *Sunday Times* journalists who had covered the race at the time. After they had reprinted the last few disturbing entries in his logbook and speculated on the manner of his death, they went on to report the minutes of a meeting of the Teignmouth Council Publicity Committee: "And his final verdict, as reported in the local paper, put the tragedy into the right perspective from Teignmouth's point-of-view. 'Despite the sad end,' Mr Bladon, the ex-Chairman of the Council, told the meeting, 'The voyage has brought up more publicity than this Committee has managed in fifty years. We have had this extremely cheaply, and I hope the town appreciates it.' Donald Crowhurst would have been glad to hear he did not die in vain."

It is astounding with what ease they could pitch one man's life against the revenue brought into their seaside resort by tourism. The language they were speaking was wildly disproportionate to the hugeness of Crowhurst's ordeal and human failing. You imagine that if you met Crowhurst in the Teignmouth Yachting Club, you might find him a bit arrogant, but, as that of a human being, alone in an unremitting seascape trying to come to terms with his deteriorating psychological state and his monumental deception, his story is genuinely tragic and existential, and leaves the aspirations of Teignmouth Council and little England way, way behind.

So we walked up the grassy slopes to the Council building and were shown the musty ledgers from 1968 and 1969. Arrangements for welcoming Crowhurst home were neatly typed, point after point, in meeting after meeting: "4. That the Council provides hardboard lettering suitably painted for erection along the Point Car Park ('Teignmouth

Welcomes Donald' was suggested). 5. That the Council erects its bunting and flags. . . 7. That Messrs. Honnor Marine be asked if they would permit *Teignmouth Electron* to be moored on their property on the night of arrival and transferred to the Lower Point Car Park next day into the custody of the 'Name It Teignmouth' Fund."

And later, after his abandoned trimaran had been found floating in the Atlantic and the real nature of his fraudulent journey unmasked: "The Council gave further consideration to the motion of Councillor A.L. Bladon that the Council agrees in principle to the boat *Teignmouth Electron* being brought back to Teignmouth and placed on show at an admission charge, the proceeds to be given to Mrs. Crowhurst and her family, and during the discussion on this item Messrs. Fisher and Parker were in attendance."

There was a small display about the event in the Teignmouth Museum—yellowing newspaper articles mounted behind Perspex, and bits of the boat purported to have been found by a local Teignmouth man, who had come across the *Teignmouth Electron* in 1994, beached in the scrub on a Caribbean island. It had never been brought home after interest in the story waned, and was then sold off cheaply in the West Indies. The second owner swore he could still hear Crowhurst's footsteps at night, restlessly pacing the deck. They had even found a stash of tins concealed in one of the hatches, only accessible from underneath the boat, so worried was Crowhurst of capsizing.

The Honorary Archivist, Nell Plahn, pulled out a manila envelope marked "Crowhurst" from her filing cabinet. In it were more newspaper articles and press photographs. She was sure there had never been a postcard produced. She showed us a painting by a local artist commissioned as part of the welcoming-home preparations. The trimaran floated awkwardly on a ferocious blue-brown sea. Crowhurst's disembodied head was painted in the right-hand corner amongst the waves. It was considered too inappropriate to have around after what had happened, and was eventually given to the museum where it has stayed, out of sight, ever since.

We visited the local newspapers, and rang up the photographers who used to work for them, but no one had any original images, nor remembered the postcard. We went to all the book shops, had fish and chips in a café in the main street, and walked out past the pier and across the shingle to the channel along which Crowhurst must have sailed on his voyage out to sea.

It was getting on for nine, and time to meet Fred Tooley. No one else remembered there being a postcard. I began to worry there had never been one. The pub was a rowdy place on the front, and there he was at the door. He hesitated before pulling out an envelope from his jacket pocket. The postcard showed Crowhurst standing on the prow of the *Teignmouth Electron*. He was wearing a V-necked jumper with a tie, awkwardly formal for someone who spent his time around boats. He was looking down at the deck. On the back, it read, "Greetings from Teignmouth the Devon resort chosen by Donald Crowhurst as the home port for his triumphant around the World Yacht Race [*sic*]." Fred Tooley could only find one of the postcards and was reluctant to lend it to me. He eventually let me take it. He told us to go and see Syd Hook, who lived in the last house in Ivy Lane. And to say that Fred Tooley sent us.

The sky was now sunset pink, but the curtains were drawn in Syd Hook's cottage. It stood next to the quay, and looked out across the yachts moored in the estuary. He didn't want to let us in. "Are you from the family?" he asked. "Are you from the family? Because I don't have a good word to say about him."

Syd Hook was working on the pilot boats when Crowhurst left Teignmouth. It was mid-afternoon on the 31st October, the deadline for departures, when he towed the *Teignmouth Electron* out to sea. But when Crowhurst tried to hoist his foresails, they were tangled and he had to be brought back in again. Syd said there was a sudden swell and his boat was that close to being hit by a rock, but they saved it. It was obvious to everyone that he didn't want to go. The boys down the yard said that the boat was just plywood. He must have known it wasn't up to it. Syd didn't think it would make it to Dartmouth, let alone around the world. He was amazed when he found out just how far it had got. "The man was a fool," he kept saying, his big arthritic fingers tapping the plastic table top. "Does he look like a sailor to you?" he asked, looking at Fred Tooley's post-card. "When we had to tow him in again, I said to his wife, if you've got any influence over him, you've got to stop him. She said she couldn't: there was nothing she could do."

Syd hinted at a conspiracy. I've heard this said since: that the whole trip was set up as a publicity stunt that went wrong. I don't know how far people will go, though, in implicating Teignmouth Council in the fraudulent records and the fake voyage. Syd Hook was convinced the whole sorry story had jinxed Teignmouth, and that the town had never been the same since Crowhurst.

Donald Crowhurst took 16mm film, made tape recordings, and kept logbooks. He got mid-way into the Atlantic before realising he would not survive one day in the Roaring Forties, let alone make it around the world. Something happened here; rather than give up, he set about faking his journey. Firstly by estimating mathematically his supposed position and faithfully recording it in a different logbook, and then by breaking off radio contact so as not to betray himself by continually transmitting through Portishead. He hung around the South Atlantic, hiding from the shipping lanes, and, at one point, put ashore for repairs at Rio Salado, a tiny settlement on the coast of Argentina, which was against the rules of the race. After a while he just started to vaguely guess his sight readings and make more and more incoherent entries in his logbook, immersing himself in Einstein's theories of relativity and his own private discourse on God and the Universe.

Meanwhile, the world believed he was making great headway. His press agent in Teignmouth, Rodney Hallworth, became so exasperated with the radio silence that he vastly exaggerated Crowhurst's progress. By June 1969, when Crowhurst's fictional journey collided with his real position in the Atlantic, and he could once again radio through Portishead, he learnt he was officially winning the race. The BBC radioed through arrangements to meet him off the Isles of Scilly.

But Crowhurst no longer knew where he was. He had lost all track of time and developed an obsessive relationship with his faulty chronometer, the instrument that measures Greenwich Mean Time on board. He began to suffer from "time-madness," a familiar problem for sailors whose only way of locating their position is through zealous time-keeping. Once his sense of time became distorted, he had no further reference point in the shifting mass of grey ocean. Overwhelmed by the enormity of his deceit and his offence against the sacred principle of truth, what he believed to be his "Sin of Concealment," Crowhurst "resigned the game" and jumped overboard with his chronometer, just a few hundred miles from the coast of Britain.

It took some time for Crowhurst's deception to be revealed. When they found the abandoned trimaran in the Atlantic, the newspapers talked of an accident, while Clare, his wife, believed he was still alive: "I am confident my husband is alive. I feel it." When the logbooks were eventually examined, the anguish of his real journey was serialised in the broad sheets.

For many, Donald Crowhurst is just a cheat who abused the sacred unwrittens of good sportsmanship. But for some, it is more complicated than this, and he is seen as much a victim of The Golden Globe as the pursuer of it. His story is about human failing, about pitching his sanity against the sea, where there is no human presence or support system on which to hang a tortured psychological state. His was the world of acute solitude, filled with the ramblings of a troubled mind.

The 1960s were a time of exploration, of moon travel, and experimentation, of pushing the limits of human experience. I do not believe anyone could have predicted what might happen if things went wrong: the flip side of success. At worst, *The Sunday Times* might have imagined someone getting killed trying to be the first to sail around the world, but not a death of such extreme isolation and distress. What happened to Donald Crowhurst was a cautionary lesson to everyone, but particularly to the press, at a time when adventure was being courted too casually, and probably went a long way in establishing what can happen at the very extremes of the human personality.

Notes

1 Nicholas Tomalin and Ron Hall, *The Strange Last Voyage of Donald Crowhurst* (London: Adlard Coles Nautical, 1995).

2 The minutes from a meeting of Teignmouth Council, 1969.

3 Quoted on the front page of *The Times* (11 July 1969).

Bubble House

I went to Cayman Brac in the Caribbean specifically to photograph the boat of Donald Crowhurst. It was the last stage of a long investigation into his strange and ultimately tragic journey. The boat, *Teignmouth Electron*, lay abandoned in the scrub on the south side, rotten and beyond repair. On an island that prided itself as a tax haven and a paradise for the rich, the boat felt like welcome neglect amidst the neat housing and air-conditioned world of the ideal holiday location.

It was on the third day that we decided to drive up the only other road on Cayman Brac. On the same coast as the boat, "the hurricane coast," this road had fewer houses and ended abruptly in jungle. It was along this road that we found the "bubble house." Deserted, and half-completed, the bubble house stood like a futuristic vision, like a statement from another age. We thought it was a temple belonging to a sect, or a church constructed by the Mafia, with the faint imprint of a cross above the entrance. We knew we had come across something otherworldly, the perfect companion to the *Teignmouth Electron*.

We frustrated our host by asking him about the boat and the "bubble house": both better concealed, in his opinion, than on show on his immaculate island, both shameful relics of fraud and deceit. "Bubble house" was the name the locals gave the construction, and it appears to have been built by a Frenchman. It was a vision for perfect hurricane housing, egg-shaped and resistant to wind, extravagant and daring, with its Cinemascope-proportioned windows that look out onto the sea. Only he was arrested before it was completed; his assets were frozen, and he was sentenced to 35 years in Tampa prison for embezzling money from the United States government.

We were happy to spend our time passing from the boat to the "bubble house" and back again, sheltering from the torrential rain in the rapidly changing weather. Nothing else on that insular island took our fancy or held our interest. And the two were somehow connected: both men involved in their construction paid dearly for their fraud, and both boat and "bubble house" seemed at home, if not altogether welcome, in their final Caribbean resting place.

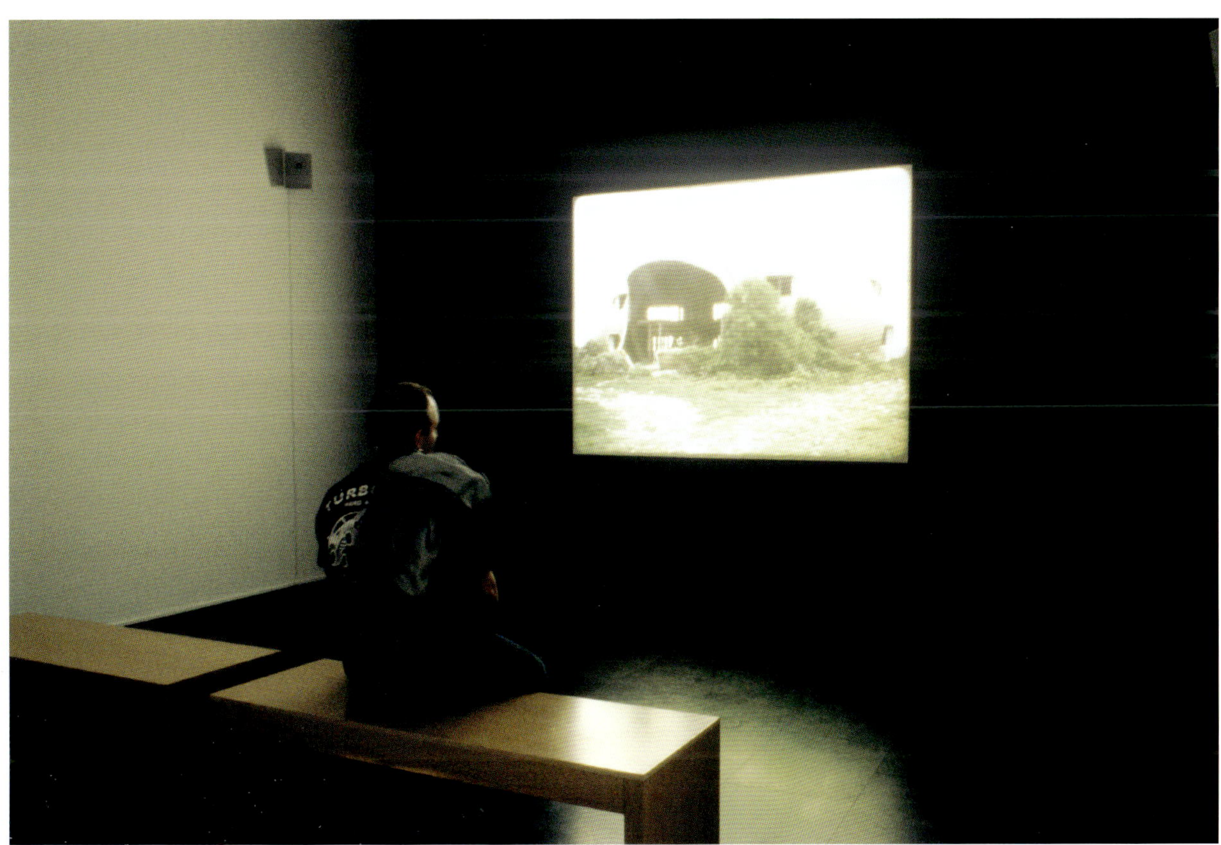

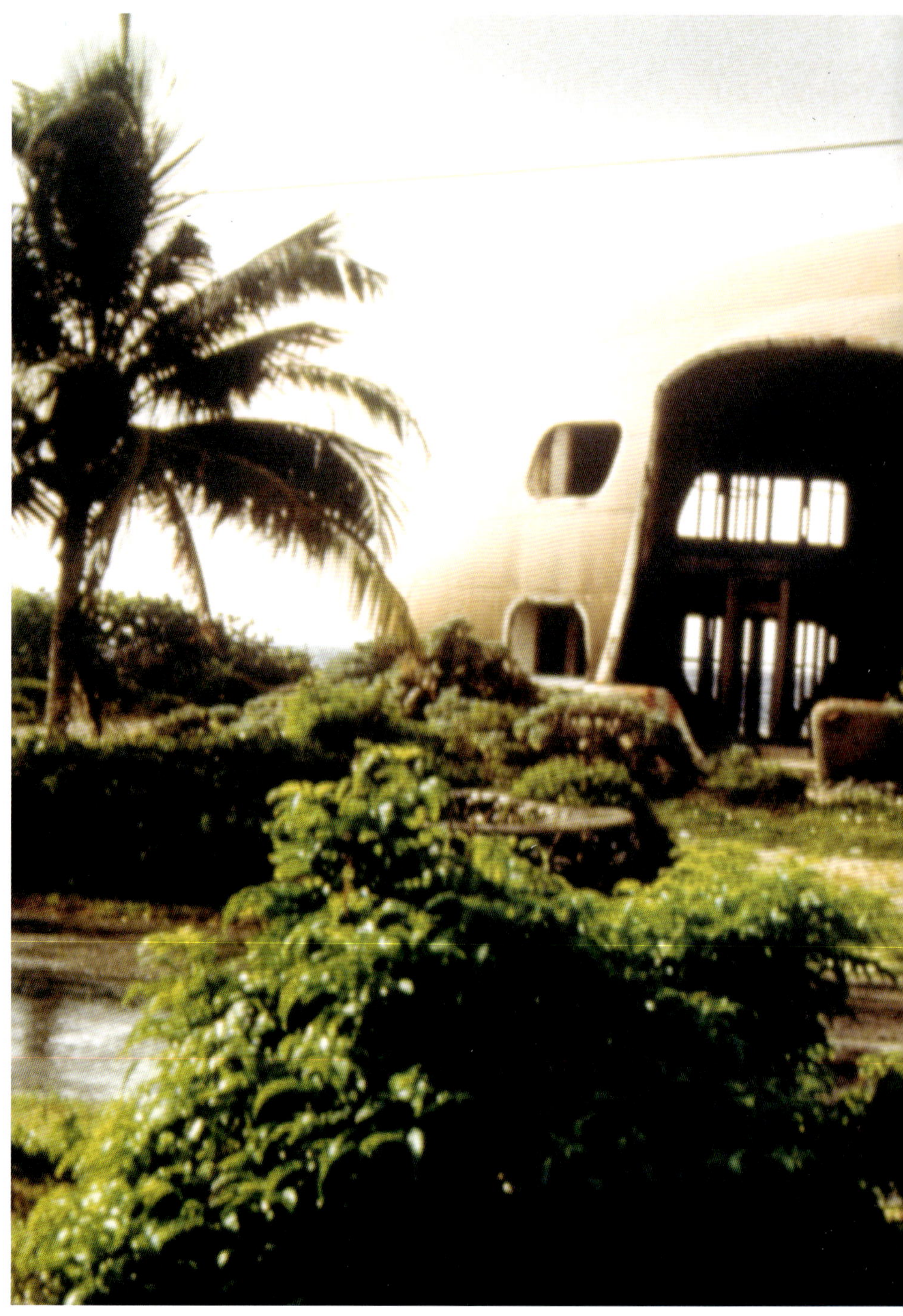

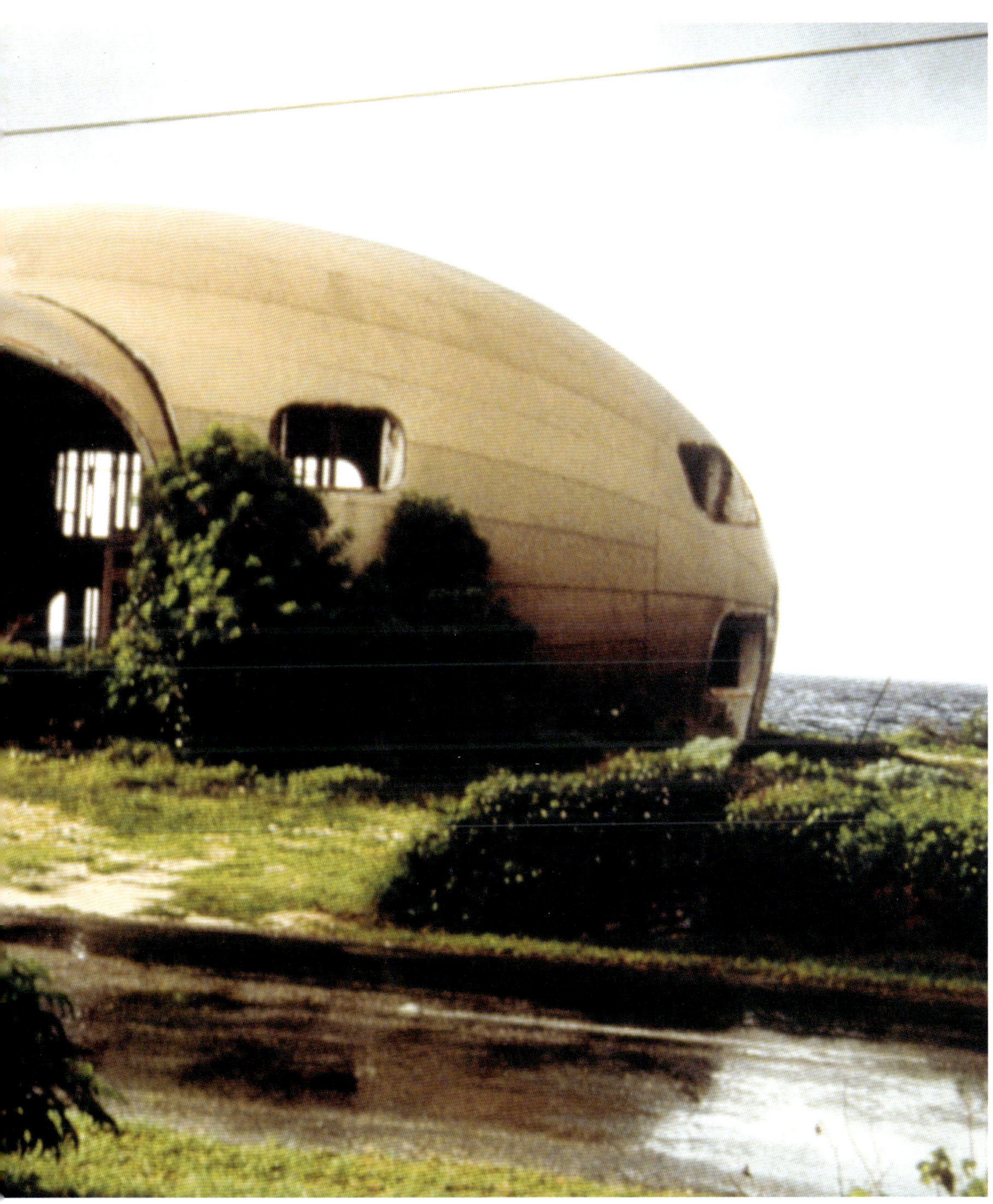

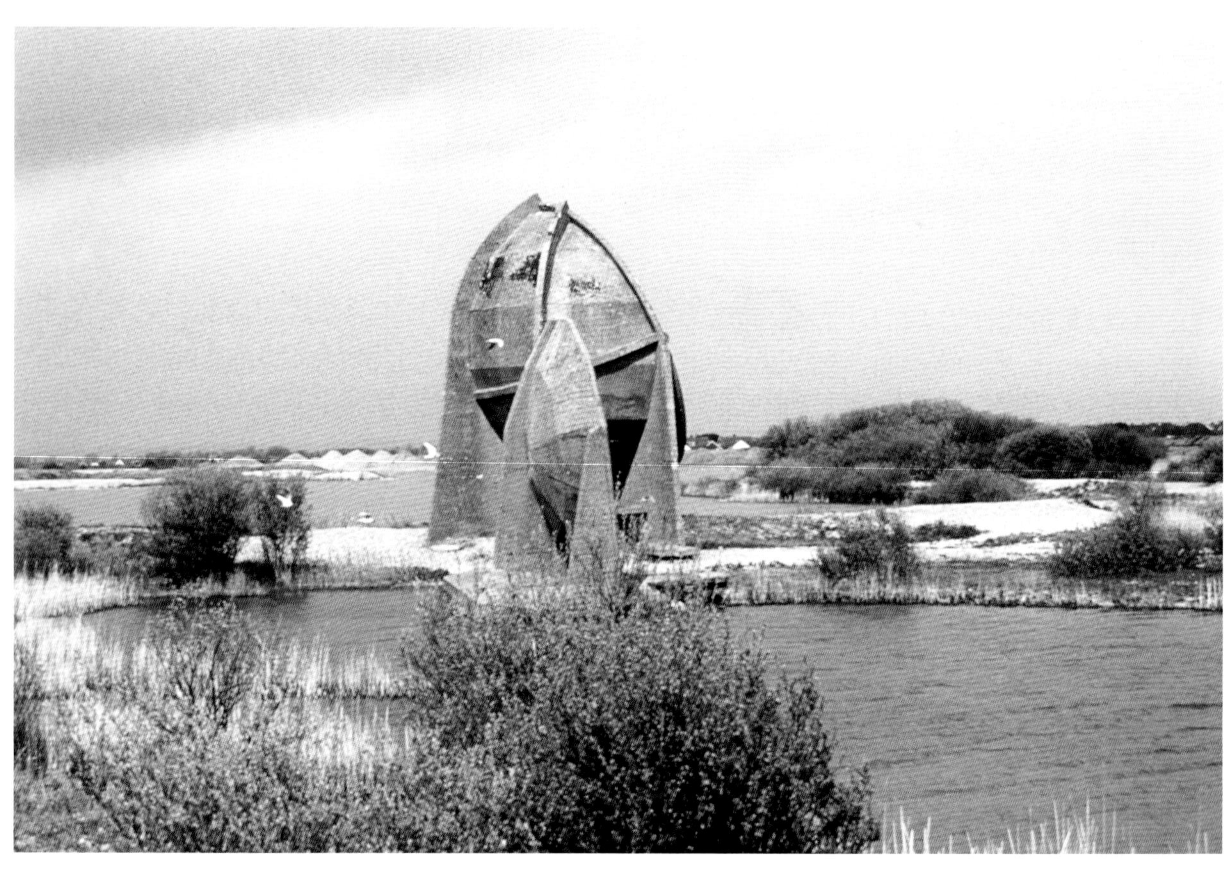

Sound Mirrors

The sound mirrors sit like big ears in the landscape at Denge, by Dungeness in Kent. When they were built between 1928 and 1930, nothing stood between them and the sea, and between them and France. Now the ground where they stand has been flooded and turned into a gravel pit. The mirrors have begun to erode and subside into the mud, their demise now inevitable. A caravan park separates them from the sea, and a barbed wire fence divides the mirrors from the holidaymakers and the weekend ramblers. To get close to the site at Denge, you have to trespass.

The sound mirror scheme was conceived during the First World War, when the concept of an air attack became the new danger to national security. The development of an early warning system became a matter of great urgency and detection through acoustic methods seemed one possible solution. A series of listening stations were developed on the south coast, using diverse methods of sound collection. Six varying sized mirrors were built on three different locations. Listeners would sit in chambers beneath the concrete structures using stethoscopes to monitor the direction and strength of the sound. The idea was to catch the vibrations of planes taking off in France and to plot their course towards Britain, having first alerted London.

Only the mirrors were not discriminating enough. Although they caught the sound well, they would also pick up any other noise, like the wind and the traffic and the propeller of a passing passenger liner, making any effective warning impossible. They persevered with them for a while, but soon they were abandoned in favour of exciting new developments with radio waves, which in turn became radar. An order to have them destroyed got lost with the outbreak of war, and these listening monoliths were spared and left to stand, solemnly eavesdropping on the sounds of Dungeness with the passing of time.

Teignmouth Electron

Cayman Brac

Teignmouth Electron seemed like the only bit of neglect on Cayman Brac. Everything else felt ordered and wealthy and fake. Our host in the bed-and-breakfast could not hide his contempt for our interest in the boat, and insisted on showing us his U.S. army service medals as alternative local and more worthy subject matter. He introduced us to an American woman who wrote for in-flight magazines because she was the one who knew all about "Winston's old boat," but we found her proprietorial and competitive, and more obstructive than helpful.

The island grew more and more claustrophobic as we sat in our hire car waiting for one tropical storm after another to pass over so we could take the photographs. We drove along every road and ate in every place. And then, we began to tire of Aunt Sha's kitchen and the same meal everyday and the pervasive scent of air freshener. We sat hour after hour by the trimaran with the airport timetables, waiting and watching for the moment when the plane was supposed to take off and fly over the boat. Only the wind would have changed, or something else had, and we would miss it again. In fact, that timetable and our obsessive desire to photograph the boat with the plane became the only structure in our day; it denoted when we could commence or abandon our vigil.

With the increasing humidity came the overwhelming desire to leave this strange and dislocated island, and a growing disquiet about its appropriateness as the final resting place for the *Teignmouth Electron*. But in truth, where the boat actually is located on the beach does have a peculiar, if unresolved, dignity, sitting amongst the Coca-Cola bottles and the broken bits of coral, with the one solitary palm tree standing between it and the sea.

"God's clock is not the same as our clock. He has an infinite amount of 'our' time."

Donald Crowhurst

A sailor's understanding of where they are is dependent on knowing what time it is. Only by knowing Greenwich Mean Time on board, and calculating the difference between it and local time can longitude be established. Greenwich is longitude 0°. Before the advent of satellite navigation, every sailor relied on a chronometer to locate themselves at sea, because the chronometer was the instrument that gave them Greenwich Mean Time. A few minutes slow on the chronometer could mean as many as a few hundred miles out of position on the map. That is why sailors are time watchers. Winding their chronometer every morning was, and still can be, the most important ritual in their day. And, if the chronometer has an error, then it is also the precision and regularity of their winding that is important, so that the rate of error can be kept constant.

From the earliest moments in his logbooks, it seems that Donald Crowhurst was worried about his chronometer being faulty and losing time. During the progression of his voyage, he became increasingly anxious about its inaccuracy and began suffering from a time madness, when he no longer knew what the true time was, and so where his position was at sea. He became dislocated, and absorbed himself in his writing and calculations, and particularly in his reading of Einstein's theories of relativity. Space and time became interwoven on a single fabric. He began believing that with the assertion of "free will," he could order the universe and become a cosmic being.

And so Crowhurst retreated into a world of abstract ideas in order to deny his real predicament in the physical world, and, being a very good chess player, chose to use its rituals to set out the rules for the cosmic game he was about to play. He stated that the game had to be played in the mind and not outside of it, otherwise it would make God sad. And, as in chess, if you anticipate that the game is finished and the outcome certain, then to play it properly, you have to resign. By the last day of his voyage, his chronometer had run down and stopped. Resetting it, he recorded in his logbook the words, "MAX POSS ERROR" and counted down his last agonising statements using chronometer time, until he wrote down the words:

“It is finished–
It is finished
IT IS THE MERCY…”

I always believed Donald Crowhurst’s life became inextricably connected with the workings of his faulty chronometer, and that is why he took it with him when he jumped overboard in the moments after the countdown in his logbook. He would have needed the chronometer with him to know the exact hour, minute, and second of the time he had chosen to resign, so he could finally commit to the end of the game. In those last few moments his chronometer, and the certainty of time, would have become everything to him.

I asked his son, Simon, if he also believed that his father had jumped overboard with the chronometer. He answered yes, that he believed he had, but to weigh him down in the water so he wouldn’t be left stranded and afloat in the sea. I remember this very specifically, because I was struck by my need to put an analytical meaning onto something that might well have been wholly practical. Maybe both are true, but the fact remains that we don’t know, or can no longer know, because Crowhurst’s preoccupation with his chronometer and his relationship to time are altogether too solipsistic and hermetic, and anachronistic in our satellite-confident age.

The Flares

“Our flaming call had spent itself. Had it set anything in the world in motion? I knew well enough that it hadn’t. Here was a prayer that had of necessity gone unheard.”

From Wind, Sand and Stars, *Antoine de Saint-Exupéry*

After talking to Winston McDermott, I went back to the *Teignmouth Electron* and stood underneath the floats looking up at the secret compartments. There were four of them, two under each side, all tightly sealed with rusty bolts. I examined them, trying to work out which ones Winston might have opened. By the edge of the front left compartment, I noticed the wood had rotted away to leave a hole. I tentatively put my hand through and felt around. Inside, there was a distinct space, full of what felt like mulch. I carefully brought some of it out. In my hand was rust. I then brought out the remains of tin cans and disintegrated polyethylene wrappings, full of paper fragments. On one, I could make out the words, "lozenges" and "Slough." I carefully placed them on a wooden board out of the wind, and carried on. I groped more deeply into the space and felt a solid object. I started, thinking what it might be, and pulled out a packet of boatman's flares. There were three of them zipped tightly into a red plastic case with a transparent cover. They had obviously never been opened, and I could just make out the words, "PAINS BOATFLARES," through the yellowed front.

I brought the flares back to England and stored them in a film can. I later gave them to the National Maritime Museum for safekeeping, where someone, who knew nothing of their history, found them by chance and called in the Bomb Squad, who had them destroyed.

I tell this story because somehow it is significant. Crowhurst had hidden those flares in the underside of his boat because he was afraid of capsizing, in which case, they would have been his cry for help. He had never used them because that was not the cry for help he needed. The flares had to be destroyed because they were unstable and unsafe, and I should not have brought them back to England for this reason. But I did, and for some short time they were in the possession of the National Maritime Museum, somehow completing a circle in the cause and effect of Crowhurst's voyage, and the incorporation and perception of it in British maritime history.

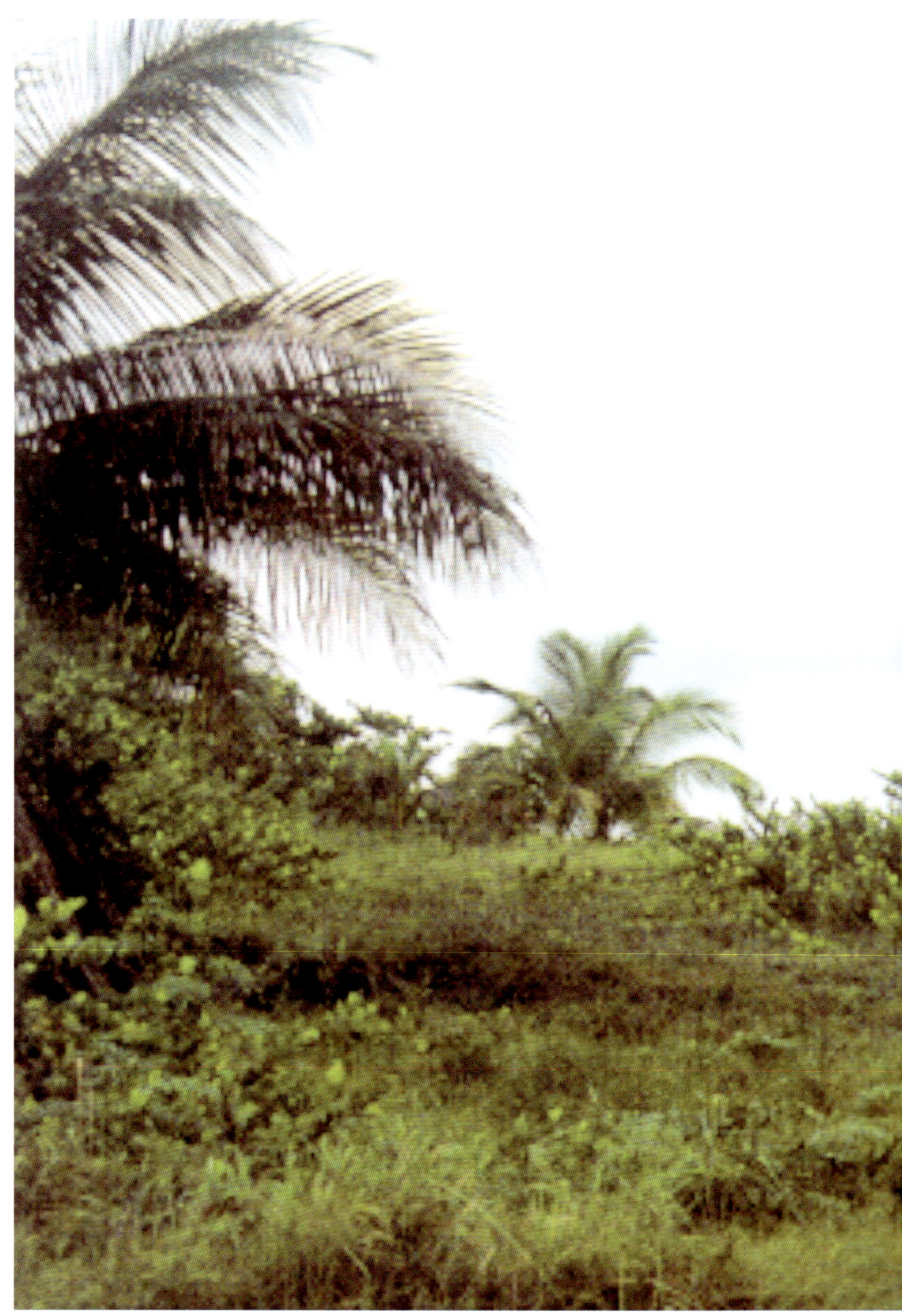

Teignmouth Electron

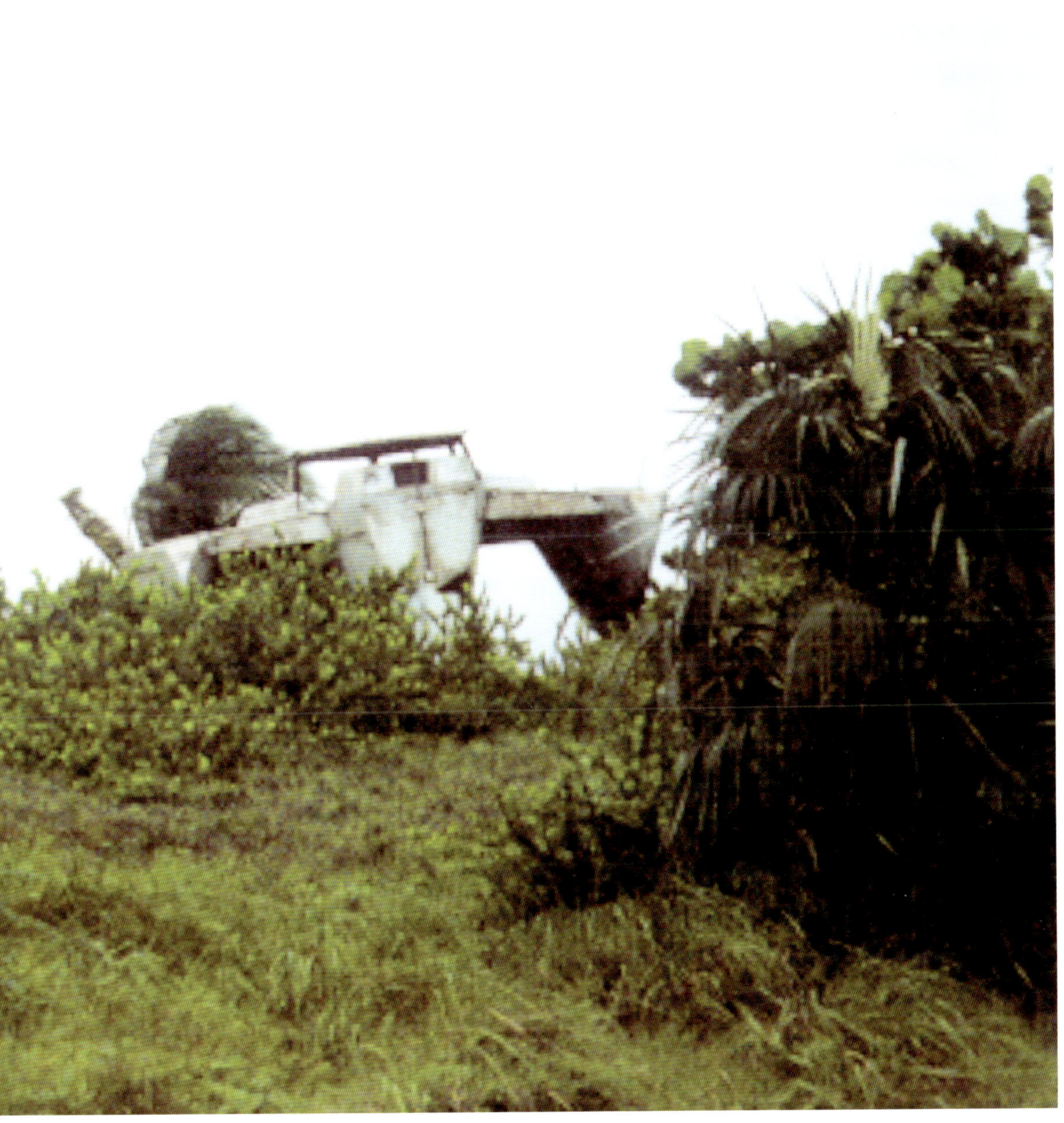

The Green Ray

When the sun sets into a clear crisp horizon, and when there is no land in front of you for a few hundred miles, and no distant moisture that could become, at the final moment, a back lit cloud that obscures the opportunity, you stand a very good chance of seeing the green ray.

The last ray of the dying sun to refract and bend beneath the horizon is the green ray, which is just slower than the red or the yellow ray. Sailors see them more than the rest of us, and they have come to signify for some the harbinger of great change or fortune in their lives. For years I have sought out the green ray, peering at horizons for that last fractional second of greenness, not knowing or daring to imagine how extravagant a green splash it might be, but never have I seen it.

And then in the summer of last year, as I set off to a small, near inaccessible village on the west coast of Madagascar to see the total eclipse of the sun, I was as much lured there by a fleeting remark on an eclipse watcher's website saying that those of us who made it as far as Morombe might also stand a chance of seeing the green ray. I learnt the night before I left, that Eric Rohmer had faked his, and that his cameraman had waited for two months in the Canary Islands for every setting sun before giving up and going home. His post-produced extravaganza was no gauge by which to measure the green ray. I had a quest to try to see, if not film, something that I could not imagine.

The point about my film of *The Green Ray* is that it did so nearly elude me, too. As I took vigil, evening after evening, on that Morombe beach looking out across the Mozambique Channel and timing the total disappearance of the sun in a single roll of film, I believed, but was never sure, I saw it.

The evening I filmed the green ray, I was not alone. On the beach beside me were two others with a video camera pointed at the sun, infected by my enthusiasm for this elusive phenomenon. They didn't see it that night, and their video documentation was watched as evidence to prove that I hadn't seen it either. But when my film fragment was later processed in England, there, unmistakably, defying solid representation on a single frame of celluloid, but existent in the fleeting movement of film frames, was the green ray, having proved itself too elusive for the pixellation of the digital world. So looking for the green ray became about the act of looking itself, about faith and belief in what you see. This film is a document; it has become about the very fabric, material, and manufacture of film itself.

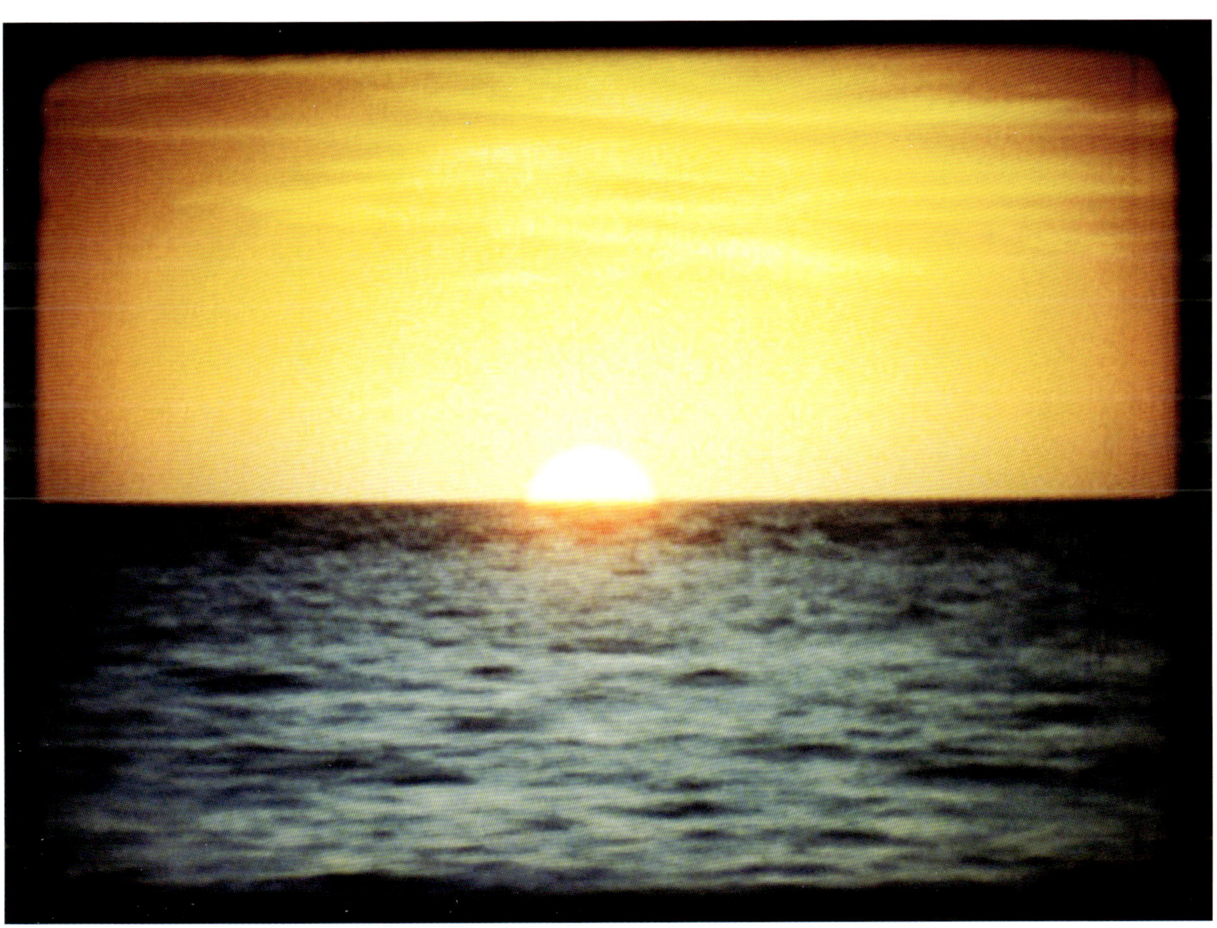

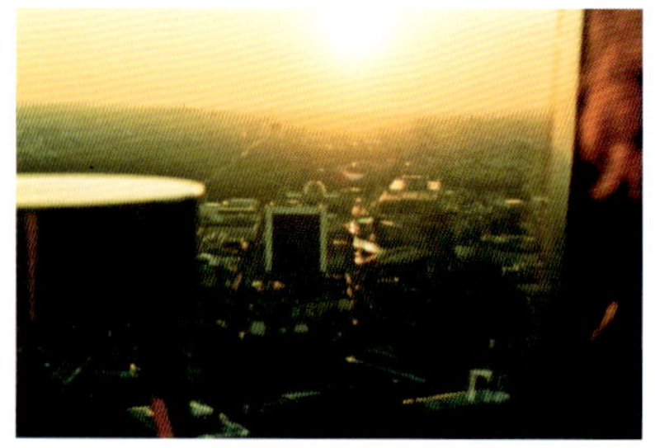

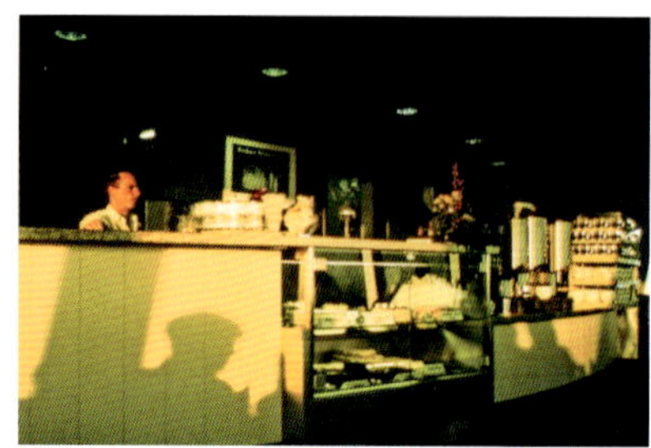

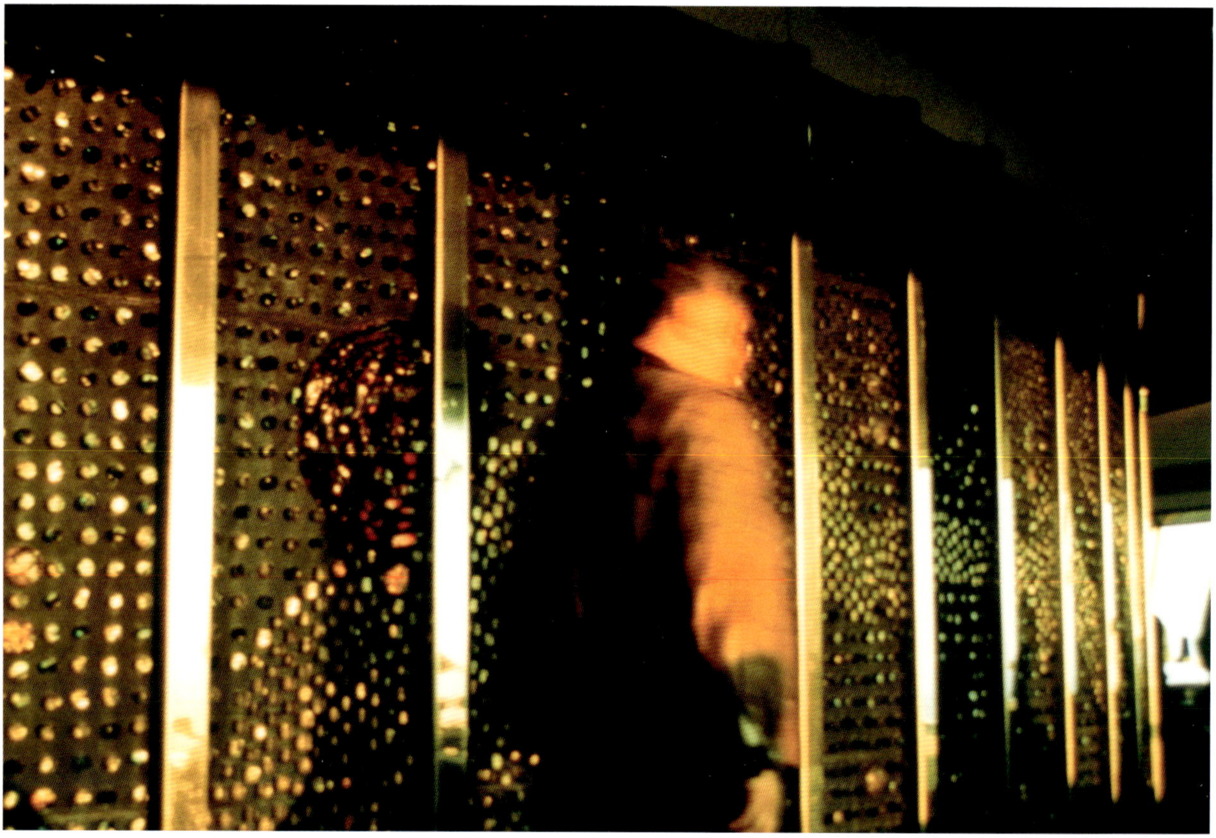

Farnsehturm, 2001, photographs taken on location

Fernsehturm (Backwards into the Future)

The Fernsehturm has become the beacon on my Berlin horizon. I look out for it wherever I am, in all weather, with its head so often lost in the low cloud or standing high above the city brilliantly catching the sun. I think it is beautiful; it excites me, yet so many people don't like it. Most Berliners from the former West have never been up it, yet large groups from the former East still book long in advance to have dinner in its revolving restaurant. The Fernsehturm has retained its political edge despite its consumption by the tourist world.

I went up it in 1986 on a college trip to Berlin. I remember the smell, the cloying cakes, and the utilitarian atmosphere of this cafe above the clouds. But I loved it. I was told recently that in those days it took an hour to do a single rotation, and that that was exactly how long you were allowed to stay there: one look at the full 360 degrees of the Berlin horizon and then out, never allowing for a second glance. There were not many public places to eat in the former GDR so a seat in the Fernsehturm restaurant was highly sought after. Consequently, it was one of the better jobs to work for the tower, so the staff were inevitably "approved by the Party." It now takes half an hour to do the full rotation. So with the progress of reunification, they have doubled the speed. And now you can stay as long as you like. But the staff, who are for the most part the same staff, still seem to work with the old system. Your order is taken and delivered with impeccable speed and efficiency. They move around the restaurant floor as if choreographed for the corps de ballet, never pausing to show disorientation or doubt as their world continually shifts and moves away from them.

Like the perpetual rotation of the spacecraft in Stanley Kubrick's *2001: A Space Odyssey*, a conceit to maintain gravity on board ship, the Fernsehturm restaurant continues to turn almost imperceptibly, like the movement of the planets in space. It was visionary in its concept and a symbol of the future, and yet it is out of date. The Fernsehturm embodies the perfect anachronism. The revolving sphere in space still remains our best image of the future and yet it is firmly locked in the past, in a period of division and dissatisfaction on Earth that led to the belief that space was an attainable and better place. As you sit up there at your table, opposite the person whom you are with, and with your back to the turn of the restaurant, you are no longer static in the present but moving with the rotation of the Earth backwards into the future.

Pie

I've become a bird watcher, watching and waiting for the magpies to land on the tree behind my studio like they have been doing lately. But tonight they are teasing me, performing some dusk ritual, swooping from one tree to another in the middle distance, unwinding, I imagine, after their long day's thieving. Sometimes I've seen as many as thirty perched on that flimsy birch or hidden darkly in the crosshatching of the scrub below it. It's where they come to sleep, if magpies sleep. Or, at least, it's where they come at night.

Magpies gather superstition. Even I find myself involuntarily saluting every time I see one alone. Everyone behaves differently; I put my hand to my forehead and mime a dry spit. Mathew, quite independent of me, intones, "Morning Mr. Magpie, I trust your wife is well." Somehow we believe this bird has the power to determine our fate, but if we defer to it properly, it will overlook the fact that we ever dared to notice it.

"One for sorrow, two for mirth,
Three for a wedding, four for a birth,
Five for silver, six for gold,
Seven for a secret not to be told.
Eight for heaven, nine for hell,
And ten for the devil's own self."

Even the Greeks imagined magpies were the souls of garrulous and gossiping women, gathering at twilight like witches to put curses on those who had failed to salute them by day. Their behavior has also been attributed to their persecution by farmers; once saucy and merry and home-loving, they have became hardened and suspicious, and shun the human gaze. They were cursed by God for not wearing full mourning black at the Crucifixion, but beloved of Bacchus for their drunken chattering selves. Even Noah threw them out of the Ark for stealing and telling tales, but they hung around and taunted him with their unending tittle-tattle.

Now it's dark outside and I can hear some of them at last settled in my tree. I am afraid they may leave soon, as they only gather together for a short while in the spring to resolve territorial conflicts and establish their social standing. Their numbers are already depleting, and I miss them.

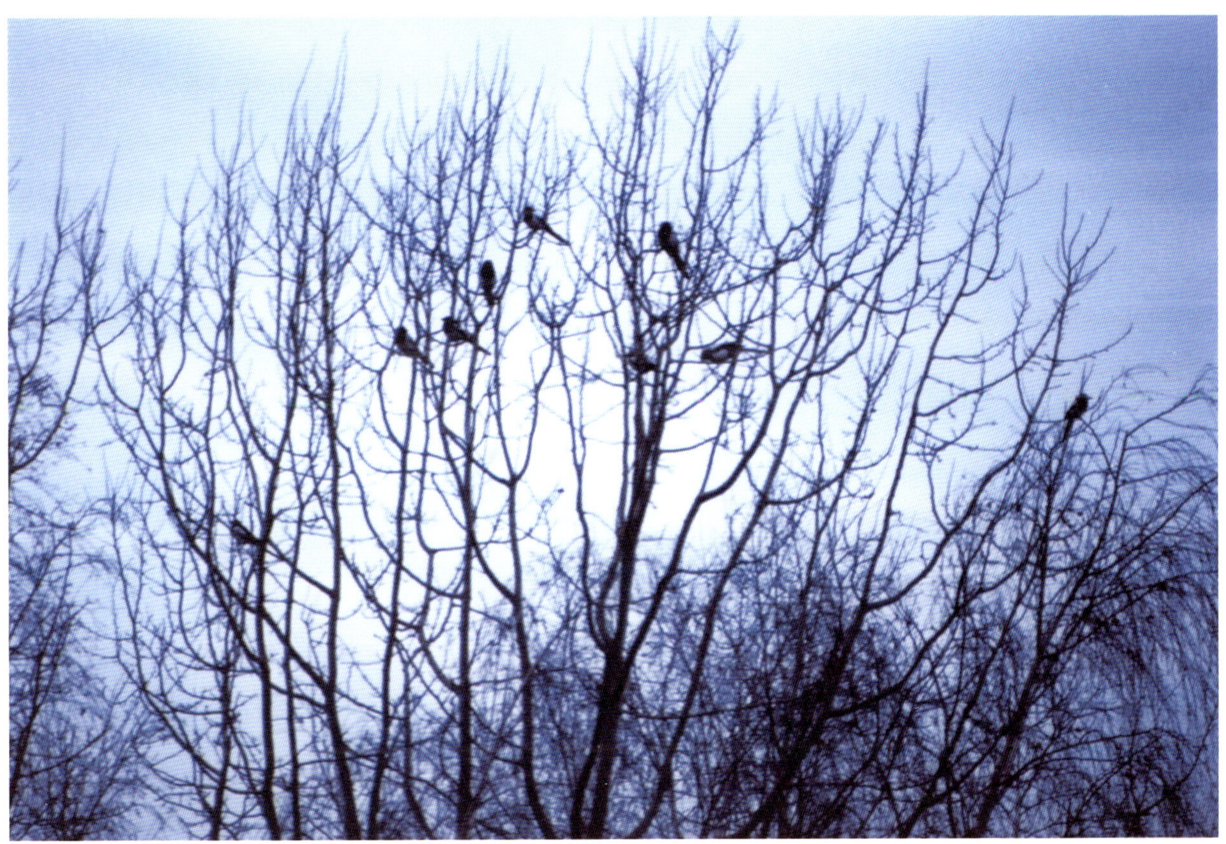

Palast

It is the building that always catches and holds the sun in the grey center of the city, its regime-orange reflective glass mirroring the setting sun perfectly as it moves from panel to panel along the checkered surface, drawing you in to notice it on your way up the Unter den Linden to Alexanderplatz. For a time, when Berlin was still new to me, it was just another abandoned building of the former East that beguiled me despite its apparent ugliness, tricking and teasing the light, and flattering the sensible and solid nineteenth-century cathedral opposite with its reflections. Only later did I learn that it was the Palast der Republik and former government building of the GDR, a contentious place that concealed its history in the opacity of its surface, but had now been run-down, stripped of its trimmings, and was awaiting the verdict on its future.

It was built on the site of a grand Baroque palace that was demolished in 1950. The revivalists want the palace back; they want to rebuild it in its wedding-cake finery and pretend it was never not there. They want to reimagine history and erase the Palast der Republik, so that we, in the future, can no longer guess at a past.

And then there are those who are fighting to keep the Palast standing, who believe to level such a building is to level memory, and that a city needs to keep its scars within the fabric of its architecture in order to preserve what our finite human memory will soon forget. Berlin needs to keep evidence of that other place, that country, and its corrupt mismanagement of a utopia that has now been crossed out as a mistake in the reckoning of history.

And then there are others, like me, who are attracted to the Palast for aesthetic reasons: the totalitarian aesthetic. We, who have no inkling of what the building meant when it had meaning, had no reason to look upon it and know the monster it contained when the copper-tinted mirrored glass was not about catching reflections and deflecting the sun, but about looking in one direction only, about being observed without leave to observe.

When the Palast der Republik was first opened in 1976, it was clad in white marble with 180 meters of windowed façade, triumphant in its transparent splendor, and so named "the house of a thousand windows." There is now no trace of the white marble; the structure is raw wood and the windows are tarnished like dirty metal. It is as if the state is letting time make up its mind, letting entropy do the job and make the decision it is loathe to make. But the sore in the centre of the city is too public and so, a month ago, the wedding cake won and the Palast der Republik was condemned. The revivalists were triumphant. Soon Museum Island will be homogenised into stone-white fakery and will no longer twinkle with a thousand setting suns.

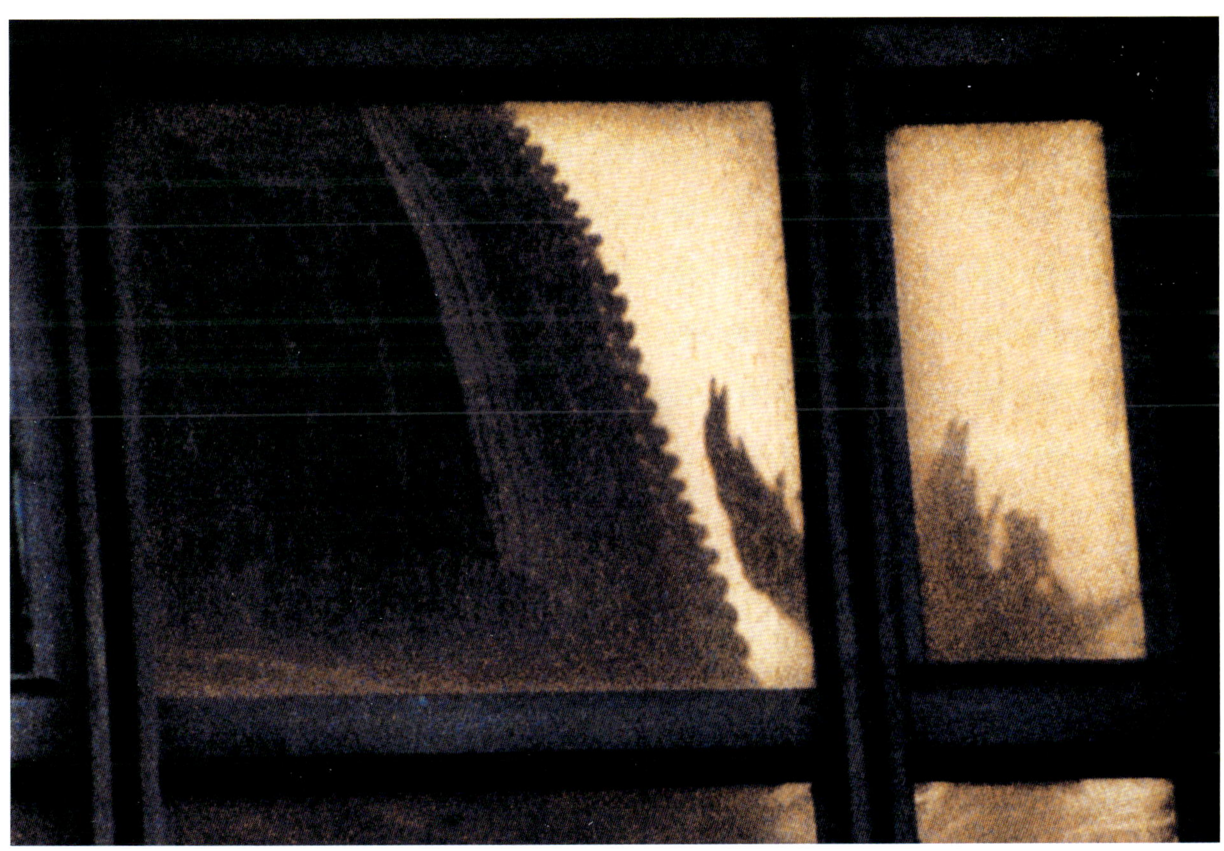

Kodak

Analogue

I realise that I do not know what analogue means. I flounder about trying to find a definition that will make sense in the context of this text, this book, and this exhibition. Analogue, it seems, is a description—a description, in fact, of all things I hold dear. It is a word that means proportion and likeness, and is, according to one explanation, a representation of an object that resembles the original, not a transcription or a translation but an equivalent in a parallel form—continuously variable, measurable and material. Everything we can quantify physically is analogue: length, width, voltage, and pressure. Telephones are analogue; the hands of watches that turn with the rotation of the earth are analogue; writing is analogue; drawing is analogue. Even crossing out is analogue. Thinking, too, becomes analogue when it is materialised into a concrete form, when it is transmuted into lines on paper or marks on a board. It is as if my frame of mind is analogue when I draw: my unconscious reverie made manifest as an impression on a surface.

Analogue implies a continuous signal—a continuum and a line—whereas digital constitutes what is broken up, or, rather, broken down, into millions of numbers. I should not eschew the digital world because it is, of course, the great enabler of immediacy, reproduction, and convenience, and has radicalised our times, indescribably. But for me, it just does not have the means to create poetry; it neither breathes nor wobbles, but tidies up our society, correcting it, and then leaves no trace. I wonder if this is because it is not born of the physical world, but is impenetrable and intangible. It is too far from drawing, where photography and film have their roots: the imprint of light on emulsion, the alchemy of circumstance and chemistry, marks upon their supports. We are being frog-marched towards its sparkling revolution without a backward turn, without a sigh or a nod to all we are losing. And that is the point, what we are losing is a vast immensity of treasure and yet we are choosing not to replace it properly. We are giving up our ability to make near perfect simulacra of our visual world, which digital still fails to replicate, despite its increasing proliferation of pixels, and we are doing so willingly.

Recently, I sat around a boardroom table with Annie Chaloyard from Kodak Industrie in Chalon-sur-Saône, and asked her why Kodak was capitulating so readily and so quickly to the overreaching digital bully, and had stopped producing film there. She replied, sadly, that no one seems to notice the difference anymore; the generation who are of an age with digital will soon never have seen celluloid film or known the photographic negative. It always takes a generation to forget.

Fortunately, there is still a demand for X-ray, and all those skills, honed over several generations of Kodak workforce, are still being employed in the manufacture of polyester film and emulsion for radiology. From a viscous blue solid to an evanescent transparency, the manufacture of film is a journey of sublime beauty, and one I would never have known were it not for its incipient obsolescence. Film is drawn as a line in endless circuits around this immense factory, pulled at great speed up and down and across rollers, outlining and defining a building and a process of immeasurable sophistication and scientific splendor. The lights were turned on the day we filmed there—*blanc*, as they said—illuminating their internal world as it is never normally seen. They were making tests with brown paper, either mysteriously for some classified experiment or as a demonstration for us—they would not say. As the paper sped through, highlighting by its contrast the habitual journey of the film, its opacity stopped the light, as if turning it off. All that was illuminated went dull and the scene became ordinary. Then the paper finished its cycle and the film and the light were restored.

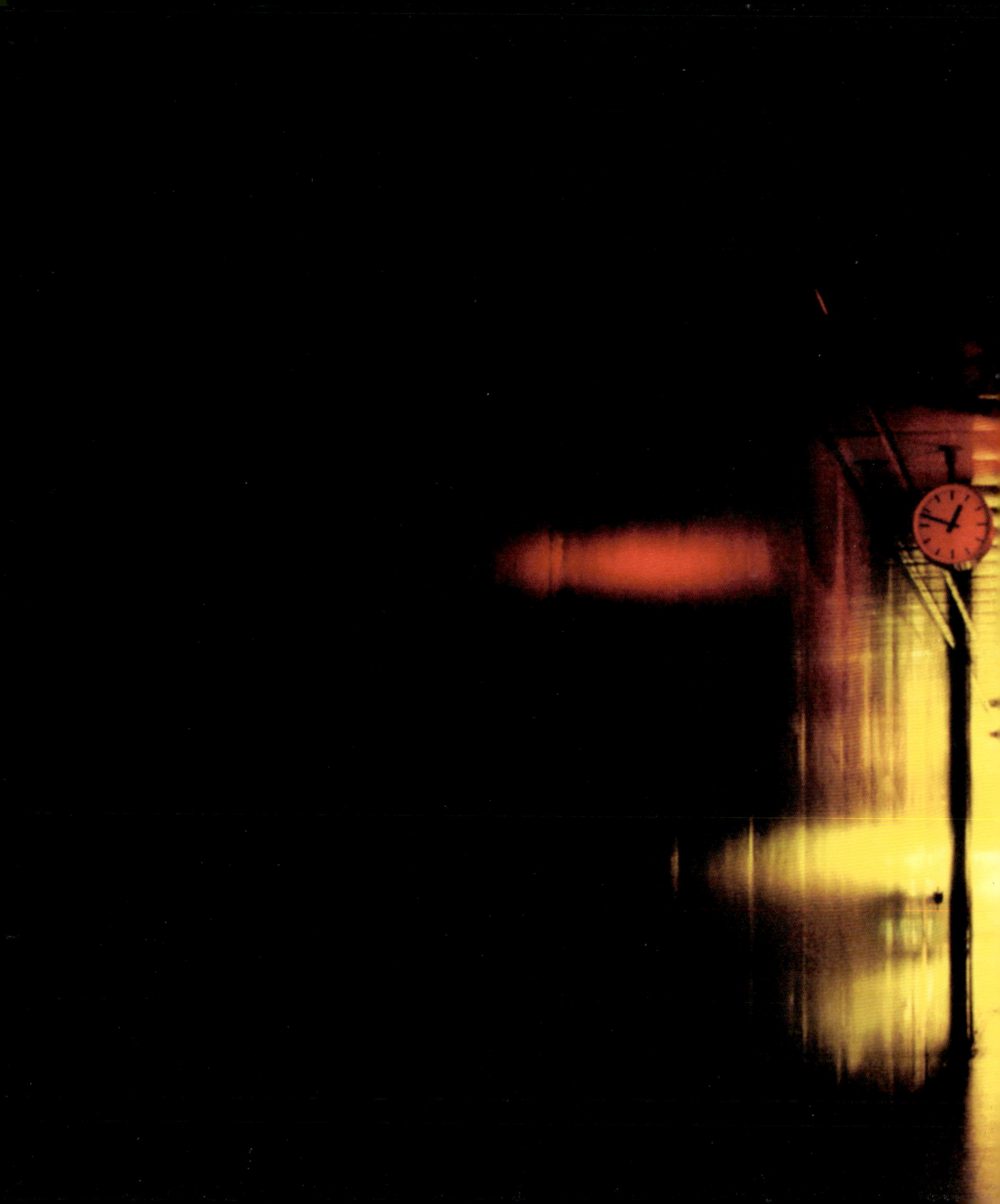

EXHIBITION CHECKLIST

Kodak, 2006

16mm color and black-and-white film, optical sound, 44 minutes

Director of Photography: John Adderley

Camera Operators: Jamie Cairney, Tacita Dean

Sound Recordist: Steve Felton

Clapper Loader: Sara Deane

Production Coordinators at Kodak: Hélène Bernard, Arnaud Denier

Sound Editors: Steve Felton, James Harrison

Sound Assistant: Rodney Belding

Digital Sound Post-Production: The Sound Design Company, with thanks to Steve Felton

Telecine: Arion

Negative Cutting: Jason Wheeler Film Service

Optical Sound Transfer: Martin Sawyer Sound Services

Printed by Soho Images, with thanks to Len Thornton

Originated on Kodak Motion Picture Film, generously provided by Kodak Industrie, Chalon-sur-Saône

With special thanks to the staff of Kodak Industrie, especially Jean-Pierre Martel, Annie Chaloyard, Béatrice Labouérie, Philippe Blot, Pascal Chenu, Didier Pepin, Philippe Rampon, and Patrick Viot; and to Anja Schneider and Johanna Wistrom from Marian Goodman Gallery, Paris

Filmed on location at Kodak Industrie, Chalon-sur-Saône

Made with financial support from Marian Goodman Gallery, New York/Paris, and Frith Street Gallery, London

Beauty, 2006

Gouache on fiber-based photograph mounted on paper, 118 1/8 x 149 5/8 inches (300 x 380 cm)

Photography: Steve White

Assistant: Jonnie Bassett

Printing: Andreas Fröbe

Mounting: Frank Lang

Transport: Günter Schlien

Painting Assistants: Emma Astner, Katarina Burin, Eoghan McTigue

With thanks to Thomas Demand and Miriam Böhm

Palast, 2005

16mm color film, optical sound, 10 minutes, 30 seconds

Camera: Tacita Dean

Camera Assistant: Lotte Møller

Sound Editor: James Harrison

Digital Sound Post-Production: The Sound Design Company, with thanks to Steve Felton

Negative Cutting: Jason Wheeler Film Services

Optical Sound Transfer: Colour Film Services

Printed by Geyer Berlin and Soho Images, with thanks to Len Thornton

Filmed on location at the Palast der Republik, Berlin

Pie, 2003

16mm color film, optical sound, 7 minutes

Camera: Tacita Dean

Sound Editor: James Harrison

Digital Sound Post-Production: The Sound Design Company, with thanks to Steve Felton

Negative Cutting: Triad

Optical Sound Transfer: Martin Sawyer Sound Services

Printed by Soho Images, with thanks to Len Thornton

With thanks to Penelope Curtis

Filmed on location at Invalidenstrasse 50/51, Berlin

Fernsehturm, 2001

16mm color anamorphic film, optical sound, 44 minutes

Assistant Director: Mathew Hale

Director of Photography: John Adderley

Camera Operators: Jamie Cairney, Tom Wright

Clapper Loader: Chris Connatty

Anamorphic Lenses loaned by Joe Dunton

Project Coordinator: Friedrich Meschede

Locations Manager: Rüdiger Lange

Locations Assistant: Bettina Springer

With thanks to the staff and guests of the Fernsehturm, especially Herr Wellner, Heinz Schulz, and Hans Jurczik

Keyboard Player: Jo Larisch

Additional German Dialogue: Karin Fiedler, Friedrich Meschede

Sound Editor: James Harrison

Digital Sound Post Production: The Sound Design Company, with thanks to Steve Felton

Edited at Thomas Geyer Filmproduktion

Negative Cutting: TKT Film Services

Printed by Soho Images, with thanks to Len Thornton

Originated on Kodak Motion Picture Film

Supported by Tate Britain, London; Frith Street Gallery, London; Marian Goodman Gallery, New York/Paris; Berliner Künstlerprogramm/DAAD

The Green Ray, 2001

16mm color film, mute, 2 1/2 minutes

Front-projected small on a wall, loop system, push-button start

Camera: Tacita Dean

Camera Assistant: Richard Torchia
With thanks to Timothé Lacroix, Agnès Fierobe, Elisa Azayou, Lolo, William Kentridge, and Anne Stanwix
Negative Cutting: TKT Film Services
Post-Production Assistant: Genista Dunham
Printed by Soho Images, with thanks to Len Thornton
Filmed on location in Morombe, western Madagascar

Teignmouth Electron, 2000
16mm color film, optical sound, 7 minutes
Front projection, screen, loop system, dimensions variable
Camera: Tacita Dean
Assistant: Kjetil Berge
Sound Editor: James Harrison
Digital Sound Post-Production: The Sound Design Company
With thanks to John Adderley, Steve Felton, David Spence, National Maritime Museum, Greenwich
Edited at Four Corners
Dubbed by Worldwide Sound
Optical Sound Transfer: Martin Sawyer Sound Services
Negative Cutting: TKT Film Services
Printed by Metrocolour
Filmed on location on Cayman Brac

Bubble House, 1999
16mm color film, optical sound, 7 minutes
Front projection, screen, loop system, dimensions variable
Camera: Tacita Dean
Assistant: Kjetil Berge
Sound Transfer: Four Corners
With thanks to John Adderley
Edited at Four Corners
Dubbed by Worldwide Sound
Optical Sound Transfer: Martin Sawyer Sound Services
Negative Cutting: TKT Film Services
Printed by Metrocolour
Filmed on location on Cayman Brac

Sound Mirrors, 1999
16mm black-and-white film, optical sound, 7 minutes
Front projection to fill complete wall, loop system
Camera: Tacita Dean
Assistants: Mathew Hale, Maya Orme, Myles Orme, Ryan Orme
Sound Editor: Paul Hill
Digital Sound Post-Production: Wexner Center Media Arts Program
With thanks to John Adderley
Edited at Four Corners
Dubbed by Worldwide Sound
Optical Sound Transfer: Martin Sawyer Sound Services
Negative Cutting: TKT Film Services
Printed by Metrocolour
Filmed on location at Denge, Kent
Made for the Public Art Development Trust Fourth Wall Project, The National Theatre, London

Disappearance at Sea, 1996
16mm color anamorphic film, optical sound, 14 minutes
Front projection, screen, loop system, dimensions variable
Camera: John Adderley
Sound Transfer: Steve Felton
With thanks to Jamie Bennett, Pippa Coles, Helen Davidson, Ian Fairnington, and Thomas Stewart
Anamorphic lens loaned by Joe Duntan
Edited at Four Corners
Dubbed by Warwick Sound
Negative Cutting: Triad
Printed by Rank Film Laboratories
Filmed on location at St Abb's Head, Berwickshire
Made for Berwick Ramparts Project, Berwick-upon-Tweed, Northumberland

A Bag of Air, 1995
16mm black-and-white film, optical sound, voice-over, 3 minutes
Front-projected large on a wall, loop system
Cast: Anthony Busi
Hot Air Balloon: Bruno Guérin, Patrick Poussardin
Camera: Tacita Dean
Sound Transfer: Steve Felton
With thanks to John Adderley, Sâadane Afif, Jean Frémiot, Vanessa Notley, Anna Selander, Brian R. Smith, and Penny Tyler
Edited at Four Corners
Dubbed by Warwick Sound
Negative Cutting: Triad
Printed by Rank Film Laboratories
Filmed on location in the sky above
Lans-en-Vercors
Supported by the École Nationale des Beaux-Arts de Bourges and the Fonds Régional d'Art Contemporain du Centre

BIOGRAPHY

Born

Canterbury, England, 1965

Education

The Slade School of Fine Art, London, England, 1990–92

Greek Government Scholarship to the Supreme School of Fine Art, Athens, Greece, 1989–90

Falmouth School of Art, Falmouth, England, 1985–88

Awards

Hugo Boss Prize, Solomon R. Guggenheim Museum, New York, 2006

The Sixth Benesse Prize, Benesse Art Site Naoshima, The 51st International Art Exhibition of the Venice Biennale, 2005

Fondazione Sandretto Re Rebaudengo, Turin, 2004

Preis der nationalgalerie fur junge Kunst (nomination), Hamburger Bahnhof, Berlin, 2002

Aachen Art Prize, Aachen, Germany, 2002

DAAD Scholarship, Deutscher Akademischer Austauschdienst, Berlin, 2000–01

Artist in Residence, Wexner Center for the Arts, Columbus, Ohio, 1999

The Turner Prize (nomination), Tate Gallery, London, 1998

Scriptwriter's Lab, Sundance Institute, Sundance, Utah, 1997

Barclay's Young Artist Award, London, 1994

New Contemporaries Award, London, 1992

Selected Solo Exhibitions

2007

Dublin City Art Gallery The Hugh Lane, Dublin

The Hugo Boss Prize 2006: Tacita Dean, Solomon R. Guggenheim Museum, New York

Tacita Dean: Film Works, curated by Rina Carvajal, Miami Art Central, Florida

2006

Tacita Dean: Analogue: Films, Photographs, Drawings 1991–2006, Schaulager, Münchenstein, Basel

National Gallery of Contemporary Art, Oslo

2005

Tate St Ives, England

Presentation Sisters and the Presentation Windows, The South Presentation Convent Sports Hall, Cork, Ireland

2004

Fondazione Sandretto Re Rebaudengo, Turin

Mala Galeria, Museum of Modern Art, Ljubljana, Slovenia

Royal Institute of British Architects, London

De Pont Foundation, Tilburg, The Netherlands

Gellért, Presentation House Gallery, Vancouver, British Columbia

2003

Marian Goodman Gallery, New York

ARC Musée d'Art Moderne de la Ville de Paris, Paris

Kunstpreis 2002: Tacita Dean, Ludwig Forum, Aachen, Germany

Section Cinéma, Musée des Beaux-Arts de Nantes, France

2002

12.10.02–21.12.02, Kunstverein für die Rheinlande und Westfalen, Düsseldorf

2001

Fundação de Serralves, Porto, Portugal

Tacita Dean: Recent Films and Other Works, Tate Britain, London

Museu d'Art Contemporani de Barcelona

Directions: Tacita Dean, Hirshhorn Museum and Sculpture Garden, Washington, D.C.

Marian Goodman Gallery, Paris

DAAD Gallery, Berlin

Under/Above, Melbourne International Biennial, Australia

2000

Art Gallery of York University, Toronto

Museum für Gegenwartskunst, Basel

Marian Goodman Gallery, New York

Tacita Dean/Matrix 189: Banewl, University of California, Berkeley Art Museum and Pacific Film Archive, Berkeley, California

Wandering Images, Sala Montcada, Fundació "la Caixa," Barcelona

1999

Cranbrook Art Museum, Bloomfield Hills, Michigan

The Sea, With a Ship; Afterwards an Island, Sadler's Wells, London

Madison Art Center, Madison, Wisconsin

Marian Goodman Gallery, Paris

The Sea, With a Ship; Afterwards an Island, Dundee Contemporary Arts, Scotland

Banewl, Newlyn Art Gallery, Penzance, England

Friday/Saturday, North Meadows Project, Millennium Dome, London

1998

Turner Prize Group Show, Tate Britain, London

Institute of Contemporary Art, University of Pennsylvania, Philadelphia

De Pont Foundation, Tilburg, The Netherlands

1997

Missing Narratives, Witte de With, Center for Contemporary Art, Rotterdam

The Roaring Forties: Seven Boards in Seven

Days, The Drawing Room, The Drawing Center, New York

1996

Foley Artist, Art Now Project Room, Tate Gallery, London

1995

A Bag of Air, Galerie "La Box," École Nationale des Beaux-Arts, Bourges, France

1994

The Martyrdom of St. Agatha and Other Stories, Galerija Skuc, Ljubljana, Slovenia; Umetnostna Galerija, Maribor, Slovenia

Selected Group Exhibitions

2006

Constructing New Berlin, Phoenix Art Museum, Arizona; traveled to Bass Museum of Art, Miami Beach, Florida

Grey Flags, curated by Anthony Huberman and Paul Pfeiffer, Sculpture Center, New York

4th Berlin Biennial for Contemporary Art, curated by Maurizio Cattelan with Massimiliano Gioni and Ali Subotnick, Berlin

Zones of Contact, 2006 Biennale of Sydney, curated by Charles Merewether, Sydney

2005

Universal Experience: Art, Life, and the Tourist's Eye, curated by Francesco Bonami, Museum of Contemporary Art, Chicago; traveled to Hayward Gallery, London; Museo di arte moderna e contemporanea di Trento e Rovereto, Italy

Truth Universally Acknowledged, Australian Centre for Contemporary Art, Victoria

The Experience of Art, curated by María de Corral, Italian Pavilion, La Biennale di Venezia, Venice

New British Art, Vancouver Art Gallery, British Columbia

Likeness: Portraits of Artists by Other Artists, Institute of Contemporary Art, Boston

Daumenkino: The Flip Book Show, Kunsthalle Düsseldorf

An Aside: Selected by Tacita Dean, curated by Tacita Dean, The Fruitmarket Gallery, Edinburgh; traveled to Glynn Vivian Art Gallery, Swansea, Wales

Bidibidobidiboo, Fondazione Sandretto Re Rebaudengo, Turin

Elements of Nature, National Gallery of Canada, Ottawa

Soul, PMMK Museum Voor Moderne Kunst-Aan-Zee, Ostend, Belgium

Documentary Creations, Kunst Museum, Lucerne

Very Early Pictures, curated by Richard Torchia, Luckman Gallery, California State University, Los Angeles; traveled to Arcadia University Art Gallery, Glenside, Pennsylvania

2004

Premieres, film exhibition, The Museum of Modern Art, New York

TIME CLASH, Fundação de Serralves, Porto, Portugal

Colecção (Tacita Dean e outres Artistas), Museu Serralves, Porto, Portugal

Memory and Landscape, La Casa Encendida, Madrid

Fade In: New Film and Video, Contemporary Arts Museum, Houston

Reflecting the Mirror, Marian Goodman Gallery, New York

2003

The Moderns, Castello di Rivoli Museo d'Arte Contemporanea, Rivoli, Turin

Trauer, Zentrum für zeitgenössische Kunst der Österreichischen Galerie Belvedere, Vienna

Ritardi e Rivoluzioni and *Utopia Station*, La Biennale di Venezia, Venice

Fotografie, Video, Mixed Media, organized by Daimler Chrysler Contemporary, Galerie der Stadt Sindelfingern, Sindelfingern, Germany

Utopia Station Poster Project, Haus der Kunst, Munich

Image Stream, Wexner Center for the Arts, Columbus, Ohio

Fast Forward: Media Art from the Goetz Collection, ZKM Center for Art and Media, Karlsruhe, Germany

Remind, Kunsthaus Bregenz, Austria

2002

Tacita Dean, Ingar Dragset, Michael Elmgreen, Maria Eichhorn, Daniel Richter, Preis der nationalgalerie für junge Kunst, Hamburger Bahnhof, Berlin

Arte all'Arte: Arte Architettura Paesaggio, Arte Continua Cultural Association, San Gimignano, Italy

2001

Futureland2001.com, Städisches Museum Abteiberg Mönchengladbach, Germany

Yokohama International Triennial of Contemporary Art, Japan

Elusive Paradise: The Millenium Prize, National Gallery of Canada, Ottawa

At Sea, Tate Liverpool, England

Under/Above, Melbourne Festival, Australia

AUBETTE: The Longing for A(nother) Place, curated by Edith Doove, Museum Dhondt-Dhaenens, Deurle, Belgium

2000

Ghosts (Loans from Nvisible Museum), Marshall Arts Drive Thru (A Delta Axis

Exhibition), Memphis, Tennessee

Media City Seoul 2000, Contemporary Art and Technology Biennial, Seoul

On the Edge of the Western World, Yerba Buena Center for the Arts, San Francisco

Tout le temps/Every Time, curated by Peggy Gale, La Biennale de Montréal 2000, Canada

Vision and Reality, Louisiana Museum of Modern Art, Humlebæk, Denmark

New British Art 2000: Intelligence, Tate Triennial, Tate Britain, London

Mixing Memory and Desire/Wunsch und Erinnerung, Kunstmuseum Luzern, Lucerne

The Sea & the Sky, Beaver College Art Gallery, Glenside, Pennsylvania; traveled to Royal Hibernian Academy, Dublin

Somewhere Near Vada, curated by Jaki Irvine, Project Arts Centre, Dublin

Artifice, Deste Foundation, Athens

Another Place, Tramway, Glasgow

Amateur/Eldsjäl, Göteborgs Konsthall and Hasselblad Center, Göteborgs Konstmuseum, Gothenburg, Sweden

L'ombra della ragione, Galleria d'Arte Moderna, Bologna

1999

Robert Smithson, Tacita Dean and the Spiral Jetty: A Program of Audio and Film at the Rooftop Urban Park Project, Dia Center for the Arts, New York

New Visions of the Sea, a commission by the National Maritime Museum, London

Fourth Wall, Public Art Development Trust, National Theatre, London

Geschichten des Augenblicks: An Exhibition on Narration and Slowness, Lenbachhaus Kunstbau, Munich

The Balloon Art Festival: Hot Air, Nanjo and Associates, Tokyo

Un monde réel, Fondation Cartier, Paris

1998

Breaking Ground, Marian Goodman Gallery, New York

Felsenvilla Baden, Austria

Disrupting the Scene, Cambridge Darkroom, England

La Mer n'est pas la Terre, Fonds Régional d'Art Contemporain Bretagne, Châteaugiron, France

La Terre est Ronde—Nouvelle narration, Musée Départemental d'Art Contemporain de Rochechouart, France

Wounds: Between Democracy and Redemption in Contemporary Art, Moderna Museet, Stockholm

Voiceover: Sound and Vision in Recent Art, Hayward Gallery, South Bank Centre, London; traveled to Arnolfini, Bristol; Hatton Gallery, Newcastle University, Newcastle upon Tyne; Nottingham Castle Museum and Art Gallery, Nottingham

1997

20/20, Marian Goodman Gallery, New York

Social Space, Marian Goodman Gallery, Paris

At One Remove, Henry Moore Institute, Leeds

The Frame of Time: Openmuseum, Museum van Hedendaagse Kunst, Limburg, Belgium

Flexible, Museum für Gegenwartskunst, Zurich

Speaking of Sofas, Atheneum, Dijon, France

Challenge of Materials, Science Museum, London

International Film Festival, Rotterdam

1996

CCATV, Centre for Contemporary Art, Glasgow

Art Node Foundation, Stockholm

State of Mind, Centrum Beeldende Kunst, Rotterdam

Swinging the Lead, International Festival of the Sea, Bristol

Berwick Ramparts Project, Berwick-upon-Tweed, England

Container '96: Art Across Oceans, Copenhagen Cultural Capital Foundation, Copenhagen

1995

Mysterium Alltag: Hammoniale der Frauen, Kampnagel, Hamburg

Kine[kunst] '95, Casino Knokke, Brussels

Whistling Women, Royal Festival Hall, London

Videos and Films by Artists, Ateliers d'Artistes de la ville de Marseilles

British Art Show 4, venues in Manchester, Edinburgh, and Cardiff

1994

Watt, Witte de With, Center for Contemporary Art, Rotterdam

Mise en Scène, Institute of Contemporary Arts, London

1992

BT New Contemporaries, Newlyn Orion, Penzance, England; traveled to Cornerhouse, Manchester; Orpheus Gallery, Belfast; Angel Row & The Bonnington, Nottingham; Institute of Contemporary Arts, London

Commissioned Public Projects

1999

Millenium Sculpture Project, London

Sadler's Wells Theatre, London

BIBLIOGRAPHY

Books and Exhibition Catalogues

Tacita Dean: Film Works. Milan: Edizioni Charta and Miami Art Central, 2007.

An Aside: Selected by Tacita Dean. London: Hayward Gallery, 2005.

Andriesse, Paul, and Peter Cox. *Some Trees.* Amsterdam: Andriesse, 2004.

Bate, David, and François Leperlier. *Mise en Scène.* London: Institute of Contemporary Arts, 1994.

Berwick Ramparts Project. Northumberland County Council/Berwick-upon-Tweed Borough Council/English Heritage/Northern Arts, 1996.

British Art Show 4. London: Hayward Gallery/National Touring Exhibitions/South Bank Centre, 1995.

Brown, Glenn. *Barclays Young Artist Award.* London: Serpentine Gallery, 1993.

BT New Contemporaries. Halifax: New Contemporaries, 1992.

Cahier 2. Rotterdam: Witte de With, Center for Contemporary Art, 1994.

Cahier 6. Rotterdam: Witte de With, Center for Contemporary Art, 1997.

Cahier 7. Rotterdam: Witte de With, Center for Contemporary Art, 1998.

Container '96: Art Across Oceans. Copenhagen: Copenhagen Cultural Capital Foundation, 1996.

Cream: Contemporary Art in Culture. London: Phaidon Press, 1998.

Curtis, David. *Directory of British Film and Video Artists.* London: The Arts Council of England, 1995.

Curtis, Penelope, et al. *At One Remove.* Leeds: Henry Moore Institute, 1997.

Dean, Tacita. *Die Regimentstochter.* Göttingen: Steidl, 2005.

——. *The Green Ray,* ed. Hans Ulrich Obrist. Cologne: Verlag der Buchhandlung Walther König, 2003.

——. *Missing Narratives.* London: Frith Street Gallery, 1997.

——. *Selected Writings.* Paris: Paris Musées, editions des Musées de la Ville de Paris, and Göttingen: Steidl, 2003. [This and the following six volumes were published together as a boxed set.]

Tacita Dean: 12.10.02–21.12.02. Düsseldorf: Kunstverein für die Rheinlande und Westfalen; reprinted Paris: Paris Musées, editions des Musées de la Ville de Paris, and Göttingen: Steidl, 2003.

Sebald, W.G. *Tacita Dean.* Paris: Paris Musées, editions des Musées de la Ville de Paris, and Göttingen: Steidl, 2003.

Tacita Dean: The Russian Ending. Paris: Paris Musées, editions des Musées de la Ville de Paris, and Göttingen: Steidl, 2003.

Tacita Dean: Boots. Paris: Paris Musées, editions des Musées de la Ville de Paris, and Göttingen: Steidl, 2003.

Tacita Dean: Complete Works and Filmography, 1991–2003. Paris: Paris Musées, editions des Musées de la Ville de Paris, and Göttingen: Steidl, 2003.

Tacita Dean: Essays. Paris: Paris Musées, editions des Musées de la Ville de Paris, and Göttingen: Steidl, 2003.

——. *Tacita Dean: Berlin Works.* London: Tate St. Ives, 2005.

——. *Teignmouth Electron.* London: Book Works in association with the National Maritime Museum, 1999.

Dean, Tacita, in collaboration with Martyn Ridgewell. *Floh.* Göttingen: Steidl, 2001.

De Cecco, Emanuela. *Tacita Dean.* Milan: Postmedia Books, 2004.

Foley Artist. London: Tate Gallery, 1996.

Legerstee, Hedi. *Publieksonderzoek 1997, in opdracht van International Film Festival Rotterdam.* 1997.

Mysterium Alltag. Hamburg: Kampnagel, 1995.

Royoux, Jean-Christophe, Marina Warner, and Germaine Greer. *Tacita Dean.* London and New York: Phaidon Press, 2006.

Swinging the Lead. Bristol: International Festival of the Sea, 1996.

Tacita Dean. Barcelona: Museu d'Art Contemporani de Barcelona, and Actar, 2000.

Tacita Dean. Bourges: École National des Beaux-Arts, 1995.

Tacita Dean. Dublin: Dublin City Gallery The Hugh Lane, 2007.

Tacita Dean. London: Tate Gallery Publishing Limited, 2001.

Tacita Dean. Philadelphia: Institute of Contemporary Art, University of Pennsylvania, 1998.

Tacita Dean: Analogue, Drawings 1991–2006, ed. Theodora Vischer and Isabel Friedli. Basel: Schaulager, and Göttingen: Steidl, 2006.

Tacita Dean: Gellért. Barcelona: Fundació "la Caixa," 2000.

Tacita Dean: Selected Works from 1994–2000. Basel: Museum für Gegenwartskunst Basel, 2000.

Voiceover: Sound and Vision in Recent Art. London: National Touring Exhibitions, The South Bank Centre, 1998.

Wolfs, Rein. *Flexible.* Zürich: Museum für Gegenwartskunst, 1997.

Wounds: Between Democracy and Redemption

in Contemporary Art. Stockholm: Moderna Museet, 1998.

Reviews and Magazine Articles

Aitken, Doug, and Tacita Dean. "Tarzan & Jane: Illusions." *Domus* (September 2006), pp. 122–23.

Anson, Libby. "Tim Head/Tacita Dean." *Art Monthly* (July/August 1995).

Anton, Saul. "Tacita Dean: *Banewl + Sound Mirrors.*" *Time Out New York* 234 (16–23 March 2000).

Arning, Bill. "Prize Matters." *Time Out New York* 171 (31 December 1998–7 January 1999).

"An Aside." *Frieze* (May 2005).

Brownrigg, Silvia. "Interview with a Dead Deceiver." *Frieze* (March/April 1998).

Burton, Johanna. "Tacita Dean: 'The Russian Ending.'" *Time Out New York* 332 (7–14 February 2002).

Campbell, Jim. "Tacita Dean: The Artist as Narrator." *Contemporary Visual Arts* 34 (Summer 2001), pp. 46–51.

Carabell, Paula. "Sound as Duration in the Films of Tacita Dean." *Parkett* 62 (2001), pp. 36–45.

Cereijido, Fabian. "Just Because Nobody Claims to Be Able to Bring You the Future Doesn't Mean that It Isn't Coming. . . " *Flash Art* (June 1998) pp. 65–67.

Chang, Chris. "Tacita Dean." *Film Comment* (May/June 2002).

Coleman, Nick. "The Artist in Clover." *The Independent on Sunday* (17 October 2004), pp. ABC10–12.

Cork, Richard. "Canvassing Our Brightest Talent." *The Times* (17 June 1998).

——. "Out with a Clop, Whir and Clunck. . . " *The Times* (3 September 1996).

Currah, Mark. "Video, Projection, Film." *Time Out London* (10 June 1998).

Dean, Tacita. "Artist Questionnaire: 21 Responses." *October* 100 (Spring 2002), pp. 26–27.

——."The English Patient." *The Independent* (3 February 2001).

——. "Tacita Dean on the Art of Matthew Buckingham: Historical Fiction." *Artforum* (March 2004), pp. 146–51.

——. "Tristan da Cunha." *Artforum* (Summer 2005), p. 275.

——. "W.G. Sebald." *October* 106 (Fall 2003).

——. "Zen and the Art of Film Making." *The Guardian* (15 October 1997).

Dean, Tacita, and Jeremy Millar. "A Report on a Future Visit to Shepperton." *Afterall* 1 (Autumn/Winter 1999), pp. 116–119.

Deepwell, Katy. "Uncanny Resemblances." *Women's Art Journal* (January/February 1995).

Del Re, Gianmarco. "Tacita Dean." *Flash Art* (May–June 1997).

Dietrich, Dorothea. "The Space in Between: Tacita Dean's Russian Ending." *Art on Paper* (May/June 2002), pp. 48–53.

Dillon, Brian. "Back to the Future: Tacita Dean and the New Nostalgia." *Modern Painters* (June 2006).

——. "The History of Future Technology." *Tate Etc.* 5 (Autumn 2005), pp. 104–07.

Ebner, Jörn. "Aus Frankensteins Genlabor." *Frankfurter Allegmeine Zeitung* (18 October 1997).

Eugenides, Jeffrey. "Tacita Dean." *Bomb* (June 2006).

Feldman, Melissa. "Foley Artist." *Art Monthly* (October 1996).

Gleadell, Colin. "Making It by Faking It." *The Daily Telegraph* (1 February 2001).

Godfrey, Mark. "Future Past." *Art Monthly* (February 2004).

——. "Photography Found and Lost: On Tacita Dean's *Floh.*" *October* 114 (Fall 2005), pp. 90–119.

——. "Time Has Told Me." *Frieze* 88 (January/February 2005), pp. 102–07.

Grant, Simon. "Coming Up for Air." *Art Monthly* (May 1994).

Greenberg, Sarah. "Art Now: Tacita Dean/Focus on New Art." *Tate Magazine* (Winter 1996/1997).

——. "Berwick Ramparts Project: Berwick-upon-Tweed." *Art Monthly* (September 1996).

Herbert, Martin. "Tacita Dean: Frith Street." *Time Out London* (24 September 1997).

——. "Tacita Dean: Tate Britain, London." *Tema Celeste* (May/June 2001).

Higgie, Jennifer. "Tacita Dean: Tate Gallery, London." *Frieze* (November/December 1996).

Holert, Tom. "Tacita Dean: Museu d'Art Contemporani de Barcelona." *Artforum* (Summer 2001).

Hopkin, Allanah. "New Found Landscape." *The Sunday Times* (4 January 1998).

Hubbard, Sue. "Tim Head and Tacita Dean." *Time Out London* (21 June 1995).

Hunt, Ian. "Mise en Scène." *Frieze* (January/February 1995).

Irvine, Jaki. "Mise en Scène." *Third Text* (Spring 1995).

Israel, Nico. "How I Spent My Summer Vacation: Non-Site Unseen." *Artforum* (September 2002).

Jacobs, Ulla. "Best of British: Idols." *Wiener Magazine* (April 1993).

Jeffrey, Ian. "Art Charades." *The London*

Magazine (June/July 1994).

Jones, Jonathan. "New Romantic." *The Guardian* (3 April 2007).

——. "Tacita Dean: Tate Gallery, London." *Untitled* (Winter 1996).

Kent, Sarah. "Catching Clouds." *Time Out London* (23 August 1995).

——. "Role Call." *Time Out London* (26 October 1994).

Kimmelman, Michael. "London Embraces Art, Just for Fun of It." *The New York Times* (3 May 2001), pp. E1–E2.

Lillington, David. "Coming Up for Air." *Time Out London* (23 March 1994).

Lütticken, Sven. "Borsten van Sint Agatha." *Het Parool* (2 August 1994).

Mar, Alex. "Gallery Going." *The New York Sun* (23 January 2003), p. 13.

Millar, Jeremy. "Genius Loci." *Parkett* 62 (2001), pp. 22–33.

Newman, Michael. "Tacita Dean: Fictions du temps qui tourney." *Les Cahiers du Musée national d'art moderne* no 86 (January 2004).

Painter, Chad. "'Watching a Video is a Legit Date Option for Once." *The Other Paper* (25 September 2003).

Perra, Daniela. "Tacita Dean." *Tema Celeste* (September/October 2006), p. 87.

Phillips, Andrea. "BT New Contemporaries: Barclays Young Artist Award Exhibition." *Hybrid Magazine* (April/May 1993).

Poli, Francesco. "Tacita Dean: Musée d'Art Moderne de la Ville de Paris." *Tema Celeste* (September/October 2003).

"Prizes." *Art Monthly* (February 2003).

Quandt, James. "Tacita Dean: Schaulager, Basel." *Artforum* (November 2006), pp. 287–88.

Quin, John. "Tacita Dean." *Contemporary* 83 (Summer 2006), pp. 52–55.

Rattemeyer, Christian. "1000 Words: Tacita Dean Talks About *Boots*, 2003." *Artforum* 42 (October 2003), pp. 134–35.

Richard, Frances. "Tacita Dean: The Drawing Room." *Artforum* (November 1997).

Royoux, Jean-Christophe. "Tacita Dean: A Cosmic Being." *Art Press* 272 (October 2001), pp. 36–40.

Schiff, Hajo. "Elefantendung und die Brüste der Agathe." *Inhalt* (March 1995).

Schwabsky, Barry. "The Art of Tacita Dean: Ciné Qua Non." *Artforum* (March 1999), pp. 98–101, 129.

Schwartz, Dieter. "Teignmouth Electron." *Parkett* 62 (2001), pp. 46–57.

Searle, Adrian. "Behind the Mask." *The Independent* (25 October 1994).

——. "Noises Off. . . " *The Guardian* (27 August 27 1996).

——. "People Say Nothing Happens in Berwick." *The Guardian* (23 July 1996).

Smith, Roberta. "In Basel, Contemporary Art Enjoys a Bounty of Friends." *The New York Times* (6 July 2006), p. E5.

——. "The Celluloid Cave." *The New York Times* (27 June 1997).

——. "Rewards in Galleries Uptown." *The New York Times* (28 November 1997).

——. "Tacita Dean, Maurizio Cattelan." *The New York Times* (17 March 2000).

Süto, W. "De borsten van de heilige Agatha." *De Volkskrant* (30 August 1996).

Swenson, Ingrid. "A Lighthouse and Some Tapdancing: All in a Day's Work." *MAKE: The Magazine of Women's Art* (October/November 1996).

Thrift, Julia. "Beards, Breasts and Bloody Bodies." *The Guardian* (22 January 1993).

Trodd, Tamara. "Film at the End of the Twentieth Century: Obsolescence and the Medium in the Work of Tacita Dean." *Object* 6 (2003/2004), pp. 47–67.

Van den Boogerd, Dominic. "It's Real, But Very Fucked Up." *Metropolis M* 2 (1994).

Walsh, Maria. "Beyond the Lighthouse: A Reflection on Two Films by Tacita Dean." *Coil Magazine* (June 1998).

——. "Tacita Dean." *Art Monthly* (June 1999).

Wege, Astrid. "Tacita Dean: Kunstverein fur die Rheinlande und Westfalen." *Artforum* (Summer 2003).

Weinstein, Elizabeth. "Frames of Reference." *The Columbus Dispatch* (14 September 2003).

Winterson, Jeanette. "Much Ado About Nothing." *The Guardian* (29 September 2005).

Wollen, Peter. "Tacita Dean." *Afterall* 1 (Autumn/Winter 1999), pp. 106–112.

Yates, Christopher A. "Exploring Passing Time." *The Columbus Dispatch* (14 September 2003).

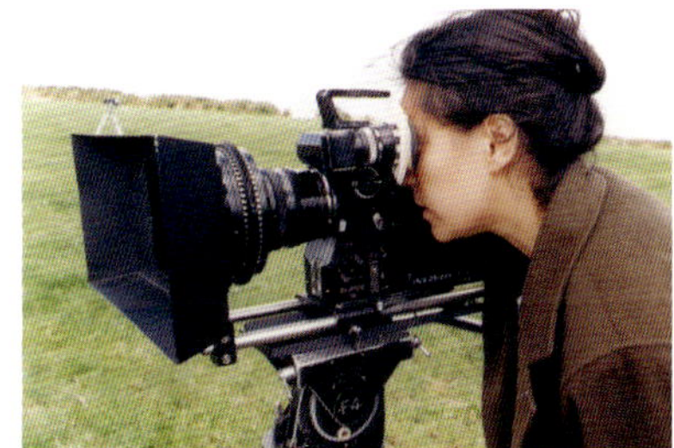

This catalogue was published in conjunction with the exhibition
Tacita Dean: Film Works
Curated by Rina Carvajal
Miami Art Central (MAC)
20 January 2007 – 15 April 2007

Tacita Dean: Film Works is made possible by The Cisneros Fontanals Art Foundation (CIFO), and through the supporting partnership of Porsche Cars North America, Inc. and Deutsche Bank. With additional support from the Miami-Dade County Department of Cultural Affairs, the Cultural Affairs Council, the Mayor, the Miami-Dade Board of County Commissioners, and The Cowles Charitable Trust.

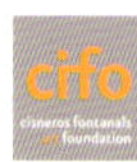

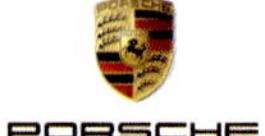

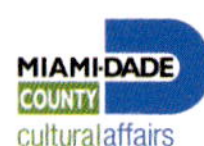

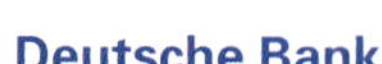

Exhibition organized by Miami Art Central (MAC) and curated by Rina Carvajal, Executive Director and Chief Curator, MAC.

The lenders to the exhibition, the contributors to the catalogue, and Tacita Dean deserve particular gratitude for their support. For generously donating their time and expertise, special thanks to: Kenneth Graham; Simeon Corless; Rose Lord and the staff at Marian Goodman Gallery, New York; Frith Street Gallery, London; Natalia Zuluaga, Curatorial Assistant for this exhibition; and all the staff of Miami Art Central.

The artist would like to thank: Ken Graham; Simeon Corless; Len Thornton; Emma Astner; Ruud & Roos Molleman; Robert Miniaci; Josefine Ciervo; Jane Hamlyn, Dale McFarland and everyone at Frith Street Gallery, London; Marian Goodman, Rose Lord, Agnès Fierobe, Catherine Belloy and everyone at Marian Goodman Gallery, New York/Paris; Rina Carvajal and her staff at Miami Art Central; and Mathew and Rufus Hale.

Edited by: Rina Carvajal
Copyediting: Joseph R. Wolin
Book design: John Isaacs

Charta's staff
Editorial Coordination: Daniela Meda, Filomena Moscatelli
Proofreading: Charles Gute
Copywriting and Press Office: Silvia Palombi Arte&Mostre, Milano
Sales Department: Antonia De Besi
US Office: Francesca Sorace

Front cover: Installation view of *Sound Mirrors* at Miami Art Central, photo: Oriol Tarridas
Back cover: *Berwick Lighthouse*, 1996, dye-sublimation print
Inside covers: *Disappearance at Sea*, 1996

All photographs courtesy the artist, Marian Goodman Gallery, New York and Paris, and Frith Street Gallery, London, except pages 20-21, courtesy Museu d'Art Contemporani de Barcelona; page 63, photo: Oriol Tarridas; 109, photo: Nick McRae.

The following Tacita Dean texts were reprinted with permission: *Bag of Air; Disappearance at Sea; Once Upon a Different Sort of Time: The Story of Donald Crowhurst; Bubble House; Sound Mirrors; Teignmouth Electron; Cayman Brac; Time Madness; The Flares; Green Ray; Fernsehturm; Pie; Palast; Kodak: Analogue*

We apologize if, due to reasons wholly beyond our control, some of the photo and text sources have not been listed.

ISBN: 978-88-8158-663-9

Printed in Italy

Edizioni Charta srl
via della Moscova, 27
20121 Milano
Tel. +39-026598098/026598200
Fax +39-026598577
e-mail: edcharta@tin.it

Charta Books Ltd
Tribeca Office, New York City
Tel. +1-313-406-8468
e-mail: international@chartaartbooks.it

www.chartaartbooks.it

To find out more about Charta, and to learn about our most recent publications, visit **www.chartaartbooks.it**

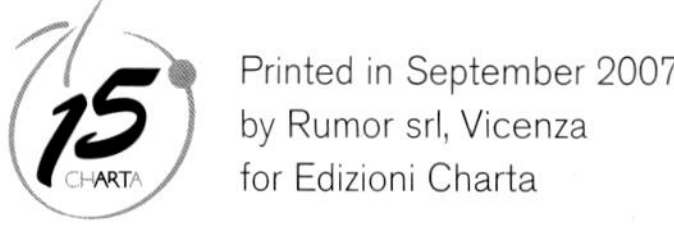
Printed in September 2007
by Rumor srl, Vicenza
for Edizioni Charta